Pharmaceutics:

A Practical Manual

Third Edition

Pharmaceutics:

A Practical Manual

Third Edition

Dr. Guru Prasad Mohanta,
M. Pharm., Ph.D., FIC.
Professor and Head, Department of Pharmacy Practice,
C. L. Baid Methu College of Pharmacy,
Thoraipakkam, Chennai - 600 097
(Former Professor and Head, Department of Pharmacy,
Annamalai University)

Dr. Prabal Kumar Manna,
M. Pharm., Ph.D., FIC, FICS.
Professor and Principal,
Flemming College of Pharmacy
Balarampur, Baruipur,
District- South 24 Parganas, West Bengal – 743 610
(Former Professor and Head, Department of Pharmacy,
Annamalai University)

PharmaMed Press
An Imprint of BSP Books Pvt. Ltd.
4-4-309/316, Giriraj Lane,
Sultan Bazar, Hyderabad - 500 095.

Pharmaceutics: A Practical Manual, Third Edition

by **Guru Prasad Mohanta and Prabal Kumar Manna**

Published by

PharmaMed Press

An Imprint of BSP Books Pvt. Ltd.

4-4-309/316, Giriraj Lane, Sultan Bazar, Hyderabad - 500 095.

Phone: 040-23445688; Fax: 91+40-23445611

E-mail: info@pharmamedpress.com

www.pharmamedpress.com/pharmamedpress.net

ISBN: 978-93-48734-98-3 (Hardback)

Dedicated to

Late Reena Mohanta

You have been the inspiration to all my work and life.

- Guru Prasad Mohanta

Preface to Third Edition

"No man ever reached to excellence in any one art or profession without having passed through the slow and painful process of study and preparation."

- Horace

It is now a decade since we had authored the earlier version of the manual. It was then meant for Pharm D Programme. We have received overwhelming support from students and teachers. We are thankful to all of them.

We have now expanded it incorporating B. Pharm. Practical.

Hope the new version of the text would be useful equally and would be liked by students and teaches. We shall be glad to receive your opinion for improving the text.

We express our thanks to Mr. Anil Shah of PharmaMed Press for his support.

- Guru Prasad Mohanta & Prabal Kumar Manna

Preface to First Edition

"Tell me and I will forget, Show me and I will remember, Involve me and I will understand".

- Confucius

The Doctor of Pharmacy (PharmD) programme is introduced into the country in an effort to develop human resources who would be able to provide pharmaceutical care on par with the pharmacists of the developed countries. The majority of the students who have been joining for this programme after +2 Science schooling are by choice and not by default. This extremely talented group of students aspiring to become the new generation pharmacists does need extreme care and encouragement during their course of study to make them competent.

There has been the real crisis often as many of the teachers even with Pharmacy Practice background find difficult to cope up with the programme. The books are not available and what are available are either not suitable or not affordable. The first year students who have just joined for the programme find it difficult to do the practical. The pharmaceutics practical though not new in pharmacy, the pharmaceutics of B. Pharm. curriculum and PharmD curriculum have different approaches. While the former has industrial orientation, the latter is practice oriented.

We have made an attempt to develop the practical text of pharmaceutics for first year students of PharmD to help both the students and the teachers. Bearing in mind the new entrants to the pharmacy programme, the practicals are written using simple languages without much medical and pharmaceutical jargon. Looking into the needs of the students each exercise is discussed to give them practice orientation. The question and answer section would help the students to grasp the subject better as well as to prepare for *viva voce* in the practical examination. In addition, the stipulated experiments, few other experiments are included for better understanding of the procedures in pharmaceutics.

We wish to express our thanks to the University Authorities for permitting to write this practical text. We thank our family members for their encouragement and sparing us from other domestic compulsions to complete this work. It would have not been possible without their support.

Last but not the least, we express our thanks to Mr. Anil Shah of BSP Books Private Limited for agreeing to bring this text in a short time.

We solicit the suggestion and criticism for further improvement of the text.

Guru Prasad Mohanta
[gpmohanta@hotmail.com]

and

Prabal Kumar Manna
[pkmanna@rediffmail.com]

Contents

CHAPTER - 1

Systems of Measurement, Storage Conditions and Common Household Measures

Like other field of sciences, it is accepted to use International System (SI) of Units in pharmaceutical sciences and practice. The few relevant fundamental units are:

Parameter	Unit
Length	meter (m)
Mass	kilogram (kg)
Volume (capacity)	cubic meter (m^3)
Temperature	kelvin (K)
Amount of substance	mole (mol)
Radio activity	becquerel (Bq)

Though SI units are expected to be used, still it is found to have the common (older systems) units in daily practice. Hence, it is essential that the pharmacist should know the common units too and their equivalents, how to convert them to SI units and vice versa.

Volume

The volume is commonly expressed in terms of millilitre (ml) or litre.

$$1 \text{ litre} = 1000 \text{ ml} = 1 \text{ dm}^3$$

Concentration expressed in gram per litre = g/dm^3

Mass

The mass is commonly expressed as milligram (mg) or gram (g).

1 kilogram (kg) = 1000 g

1 g = 1000 mg

1 mg = 1000 microgram (μg)

The 'curie' is the traditional unit of radioactivity (Ci) = 3.7×10^{10} Bq

Intersystem Conversion Equivalents

Weight measure (mass)	Liquid measure (volume)
1 kg = 2.2 pounds (lb) 1 lb = 453.4 g 1 ounce (oz) = 28.35 g 1 grain (gr) = 64.8 mg (app. 65 mg) 1 g = 15.432 gr	1 ml = 16.23 minims (m) 1 minim = 0.06 ml (app.) 1 fluid ounce = 29.57 ml (app. 30 ml) 1 pint (pt) = 473 ml 1 gallon (gal) USA= 3785 ml 1 gallon (gal) UK = 4546 ml

Storage Conditions (NFI 2016)

Storage	Meaning
Store in Cold Place	2 – 8 °C (Keep in Refrigerator)
Store in Cool Place	10 – 25 °C
Do not store over 8 °C	Keep in Refrigerator, but not in freezer.
Do not store over 30 °C	Store at Room Temperature
Protect from Moisture	Store in normal humidity at room temperature (Relative Humidity less than 60 %.
Protect from Light	Light resistant cupboard / drawer (Amber coloured bottle is usually provided for liquids)

Common Household Measures

Domestic Measure	Volume
1 tumblerful	240 ml
1 teacupful	120 ml
1 wine glass	60 ml
1 tablespoonful	15 ml
1 teaspoonful	5 ml

CHAPTER - 2

Labelling of Medicines

The labels on medicinal products are essential for identifying the product and to ensure correct use of medicines. The label should comply with the legal requirements and contains information to ensure user for appropriate use. The label needs to be neat, legible and attractive.

The label of dispensed medicines must have the following information:

- The name and address of the supplier
- The name of the patient and the quantity of medicine
- The number representing the serial number of the entry in the prescription register
- The dose (for internally used medicines)
- "For External Use Only" if the medicine is meant for external application.

In addition to the above mandatory requirements, the following information may be necessary in the label:

- Keep in a refrigerator – for medicines which get deteriorated at room temperature.
- For rectal use only – for suppositories, enemas.
- For vaginal use only – for vaginal tablets and pessaries.
- Not to be taken – for gargle, mouth wash.
- Shake well before use – for suspensions and emulsions.
- To be sipped and swallowed slowly without water – for linctus.
- "Flammable – Keep away from naked flame" – for spirits and alcohol based solutions.
- Do not apply to the broken skin – for liniments.
- Keep out of reach of children – for all medicines.

CHAPTER - 3

Syrups

Syrups are concentrated aqueous preparations of sugar or sugar substitutes. They are the pleasant liquid dosage forms of unpleasant or disagreeable taste medications. They are particularly useful for administering the medications to children.

Sucrose is the most frequently used sugar in the preparation of syrups. In some situations other sugars like dextrose or non-sugars like sorbitol, glycerine and propylene glycol are used. For diabetic patients syrups are made with methyl cellulose and hydroxyl ethyl cellulose.

As the syrups are viscous in nature, only a portion of the dissolved medicaments come in contact with the taste buds while swallowing. The remainder of the drug is swallowed without contacting taste buds. This viscous property of syrup masks the taste of the drug.

The syrups can be prepared by any of the three methods:

Dissolving the materials (Syrup IP, Orange Syrup);

Extraction (Syrup of Tolu) and Chemical Reaction (Compound Syrup of Ferrous Phosphate).

Experiment - 1

Syrup IP [1966]

Objective: To prepare 50 g of Syrup.

Principle: This is just a solution of 66.7% (w/w) Sucrose (Sugar) in water. This requires heating of sucrose and water mixture to dissolve the high amount of sucrose. As the concentration of sucrose is expressed in percent (w/w), the final solution should be adjusted to the required weight. However, as liquids are easier to measure than weighing them, using density they can be converted to volume for convenience.

Formula

Ingredients	Master Formula	Working Formula	
Sucrose	667 g	$\frac{667\ g}{1000\ g} \times 50\ g = 33.35\ g$	50 g syrup is equal to [taking density of the syrup 1.32 g/ml] 37.88 ml
Purified Water q.s. to	1000 g	50 g [Water quantity required is 50 – 33.35 = 16.65 g = app 17 ml]	

Procedure: The required quantity of sucrose and water are mixed and heated on a water bath with occasional stirring to dissolve sucrose. Finally sufficient boiling water is added to make the required volume.

Storage: It should be stored in a well closed container in a cool place.

Category: Pharmaceutical Aid.

Discussion: The Syrup IP is also commonly known as Simple Syrup as it does not contain any medicament. The heating of sucrose and water mixture facilitates rapid solution. While heating, there may be possibility of overheating. Overheating may cause a hydrolytic reaction called inversion producing invert sugar.

$$\text{Sucrose} + \text{Water} \xrightarrow{\text{Heat}} \text{Dextrose} + \text{Levulose}$$

The combination of two mono-saccharides [Dextrose and Levulose] is invert sugar and the invert sugar is sweeter than sucrose. Overheating makes colourless syrup dark due to the effect of heat on levulose portion of invert sugar.

The Simple Syrup can also be prepared by percolation of sugar with purified water (Syrup USP).

This is used as vehicle for preparing medicated syrups.

Questions and Answers

1. What is the percentage of Sucrose in Syrup?

   Answer: 66.7 % (w/w) in Syrup IP. The Syrup USP has a different strength of Sucrose. It contains 85 % (w/v) of Sucrose corresponding to 64. 74 % (w/w). This shows the Syrup IP is more concentrated than Syrup USP.

2. Why syrups do not need additional preservatives?

   Answer: The concentrated sugar solutions do not support the growth of microbes. No free water is available for their growth. They have high osmotic pressure.

   Bacteria always maintain high osmolarity well above the medium. If the internal osmotic pressure falls below the external osmotic pressure; water leaves the cell causing damage to the membranes.

   As the syrups do not support the microbial growth due to their high osmotic pressure, there is no need for additional preservatives.

Experiment - 2

Ephedrine Hydrochloride Syrup NF

Objective: To prepare and dispense 50 ml syrup of ephedrine hydrochloride.

Principle: This is just a solution of 0.4% (w/v) ephedrine hydrochloride in simple syrup.

Formula

Ingredients	Master Formula	Working Formula
Ephedrine Hydrochloride	400 mg	$\frac{400\ \text{mg}}{100\ \text{ml}} \times 50\ \text{ml} = 200\ \text{mg}$
Syrup q. s. to	100 ml	50 ml

Procedure: The required quantity of ephedrine hydrochloride is dissolved in 50 ml of syrup.

Storage: It should be stored in a well closed container in a cool place.

Category: Bronchodilator.

Dose: 5 to 10 ml every four hour.

Questions and Answers

1. What is the percentage of ephedrine hydrochloride in ephedrine hydrochloride syrup?

   Answer: 0.4 % (w/v).

2. What is the use of ephedrine hydrochloride syrup?

   Answer: This can be sued as bronchodilator in the treatment of bronchial asthma. Ephedrine is also used as nasal drop for treating nasal congestion.

3. What patient guidance required while dispensing this syrup?

   Answer:

   - Measure the dose using the measuring spoon or devise supplied.
   - Do not exceed the dose.
   - If you miss the dose, take as soon as you remember if it is within one hour. Do not double the dose.

Experiment - 3

Syrup of Vasaka IP (1966)

Objective: To prepare and dispense 50 ml syrup of vasaka.

Principle: This is a solution of vasaka liquid extract in simple syrup.

Formula

Ingredients	Master Formula	Working Formula
Vasaka liquid extract	500 ml	$\frac{500\ \text{ml}}{1000\ \text{ml}} \times 50\ \text{ml} = 25\ \text{ml}$
Glycerine	100 ml	$\frac{100\ \text{ml}}{1000\ \text{ml}} \times 50\ \text{ml} = 5\ \text{ml}$
Syrup q. s. to	1000 ml	50 ml

Procedure: The required quantity of vasaka liquid extract and glycerine are mixed. Then it is diluted with syrup to make 50 ml.

Storage: It should be stored in a well closed container in a cool place.

Category: Expectorant.

Dose: 2 to 4 ml.

Questions and Answers

1. What is the use of syrup of vasaka?

   Answer: This can be sued as expectorant in productive cough.

2. What patient guidance required while dispensing this syrup?

   Answer:

   - Measure the dose using the measuring spoon or devise supplied.
   - Do not exceed the dose.
   - If you miss the dose, take as soon as you remember if it is within one hour. Do not double the dose.

Experiment - 4

Orange Syrup BPC (1973)

Objective: To prepare 50 ml orange syrup.

Principle: This is a solution of orange tincture in syrup.

Formula

Ingredients	Master Formula	Working Formula
Orange Tincture	60 ml	$\frac{600 \text{ ml}}{1000 \text{ ml}} \times 50 \text{ ml} = 3 \text{ ml}$
Syrup q. s. to	1000 ml	50 ml

Procedure: The required quantity of orange tincture is diluted with sufficient syrup to make 50 ml.

Storage: It should be stored in a well closed container in a cool place.

Category: Flavour, Carminative and Aromatic.

Dose: 2.5 to 5 ml.

Questions and Answers

1. What is the use of orange syrup?

   Answer: This is mainly used as flavouring agent in pharmaceutical preparations (oral liquids).

Experiment - 5

Compound Ferrous Phosphate Syrup IP (1955)

Objective: To prepare 50 ml Compound Ferrous Phosphate Syrup.

Principle: The Syrup of Ferrous Phosphate is solution of Ferrous Phosphate in a syrupy base and ferrous phosphate is prepared *in situ* by reaction of iron and phosphoric acid. Also, the preparation contains acid phosphate of calcium, potassium and sodium. These are too prepared by chemical reactions. The product is suitably flavoured and coloured.

Formula

Ingredients	Master Formula	Working Formula
Iron turnings	4.3 g	$\frac{4.3\ g}{1000\ ml} \times 50\ ml = 0.215\ g = 215\ mg$
Phosphoric acid	48 ml	$\frac{48\ ml}{1000\ ml} \times 50\ ml = 2.4\ ml$
Calcium carbonate	13.6 g	$\frac{13.6\ g}{1000\ ml} \times 50\ ml = 0.68\ g = 680\ mg$
Potassium bicarbonate	1 g	$\frac{1\ g}{1000\ ml} \times 50\ ml = 0.05\ g = 50\ mg$
Sodium phosphate	1 g	$\frac{1\ g}{1000\ ml} \times 50\ ml = 0.05\ g = 50\ mg$
Cochineal	3.5 g	$\frac{3.5\ g}{1000\ ml} \times 50\ ml = 0.175\ g = 175\ mg$
Sucrose	700 g	$\frac{700\ g}{1000\ ml} \times 50\ ml = 35\ g$
Orange flower oil	50 ml	$\frac{50\ ml}{1000\ ml} \times 50\ ml = 2.5\ ml$
Distilled water q. s. To	1000 ml	50 ml

Procedure: The required quantity of small pieces of iron turning is added to a mixture of 1.25 ml water and 1.25 ml phosphoric acid taken in a small flask. The mixture is heated gently on a water bath until the iron turnings dissolves.

Calcium carbonate, potassium bicarbonate and sodium phosphate are triturated with remaining quantity of phosphoric acid and 4 ml of water in a vessel. The solution of iron phosphate prepared already is added to this solution.

Cochineal is boiled with around 19 ml water for 15 minutes. Sucrose is added to it and boiled again for 15 minutes. This is then cooled, strained and washed the strainer with sufficient distilled water to 40 ml.

The above solution is filtered into the syrup containing iron phosphate, calcium carbonate, potassium bicarbonate, and sodium phosphate. Then orange flower oil is added. Finally, sufficient distilled water is poured through the filter to produce 50 ml. After keeping for 48 hours, it is filtered.

Storage: It should be stored in a well closed container in a cool place.

Category: Haematinic.

Dose: 2 to 8 ml.

Discussion: The compound ferrous phosphate syrup is prepared at three stages: Preparation of ferrous acid phosphate; preparation of calcium acid phosphate, potassium acid phosphate and sodium acid phosphate; and preparation of coloured syrup.

When iron is mixed with dilute phosphoric acid, the following chemical reaction takes place producing ferrous acid phosphate:

$$Fe_2 + 2H_3PO_4 \rightarrow Fe\ (H_2PO_4)_2 + H_2$$

Heating over a water bath during this reaction process minimizes the loss of water which prevents the formation of solid mass. Loss of water is likely to cause formation of solid mass.

Addition of calcium carbonate, potassium bicarbonate and sodium phosphate to mixture of phosphoric acid and water result in formation of corresponding acid phosphates:

$$CaCO_3 + 2H_3PO_4 \rightarrow Ca\ (H_2PO_4)_2 + CO_2 + H_2O$$

$$KHCO_3 + H_3PO_4 \rightarrow KH_2PO_4 + H_2O + CO_2$$

$$Na_2HPO_4 + H_3PO_4 \rightarrow 2NaH_2PO_4$$

As there are considerable amount of release of carbon dioxide, a bigger vessel is necessary for carrying out the reactions. The reaction occurs partially due to insufficient amount of phosphoric acid. The excess un-reacted acid present in iron acid phosphate solution completes the further reactions forming acid phosphates of non-metals.

The mixture is filtered to remove iron carbide and carbon derived from iron solution.

During the preparation of coloured syrup, cochineal is boiled with water to completely extract the colouring matter.

Questions and Answers

1. What are the uses of each ingredient in the formula?

   Answer: Iron is used to make ferrous phosphate. Iron reacts with phosphoric acid to make ferrous phosphate which is the active ingredient.

   Calcium carbonate, sodium phosphate, and potassium bicarbonate are used to make respective acid phosphates.

   Cochineal is the colouring agent. It gives a pleasant colour to the preparation and masks the colour change of the syrup on aging (oxidation). Orange flower oil is the flavouring agent.

2. What is the use of syrup of ferrous phosphate?

   Answer: This can be sued as iron supplement in the treatment of anaemia. However, it is no longer used because of availability of better preparations like ferrous sulphate syrup.

3. What patient guidance required while dispensing this syrup?

   Answer:

   - Measure the dose using the measuring spoon or devise supplied.
   - Take the medicine after meal
   - May stain teeth. Dilute the dose with milk, fruit juice or water before taking.
   - Do not exceed the dose.
   - If you miss the dose, take as soon as you remember if within one hour. Do not double the dose.
   - Keep the medicine out of reach of children.

Experiment - 6

Ferrous Sulphate Syrup

Objective: To prepare and dispense 50 ml Ferrous Sulphate syrup.

Principle: Ferrous Sulphate Syrup is a solution of ferrous sulphate in syrup. The syrup is suitably flavoured with peppermint spirit.

Formula

Ingredients	Master Formula	Working Formula
Ferrous sulphate	40 g	$\frac{40\text{ g}}{1000\text{ ml}} \times 50\text{ ml} = 2\text{ g}$
Citric acid, hydrous	2.1 g	$\frac{2.1\text{ g}}{1000\text{ ml}} \times 50\text{ ml} = 105\text{ mg}$
Peppermint spirit	2.0 ml	$\frac{2.0\text{ ml}}{1000\text{ ml}} \times 50\text{ ml} = 0.1\text{ ml}$
Sucrose	825 g	$\frac{825\text{ g}}{1000\text{ ml}} \times 50\text{ ml} = 41.25\text{ g}$
Purified water q. s. to	1000 ml	50 ml

Procedure: The required quantity of ferrous sulphate, citric acid, peppermint spirit and 10 g sucrose are dissolved in 22.5 ml of purified water. The solution is filtered to get clear solution.

Then the remaining quantity of sucrose is dissolved in the filtrate. Finally sufficient quantity of purified water is added to get the desired 50 ml. After mixing the solution may be filtered through a pledget of cotton.

Storage: It should be stored in a well closed container in a cool place.

Category: Haematinic.

Dose: 10 ml twice daily.

Discussion: The sucrose is added in two steps. The first portion of sucrose is added in the beginning to provide a reducing environment. The reducing environment prevents the oxidation of Fe^{++} to Fe^{+++} which is likely to precipitate from solution as a basis ferric salt. The entire amount if used at this time, the solution would become more viscous with difficulty in filtration.

Sucrose may be substituted in whole or in part by sorbitol, a mixture of sorbitol and glycerine.

Questions and Answers

1. What is the percentage of ferrous sulphate in the syrup?

   Answer: 4% w/v.

2. What are the uses of each ingredient of the formula?

   Answer: Ferrous sulphate is the medicament (haematinic). Citric acid is to chelate the ferric ions normally present in the ferrous sulphate to prevent them from forming insoluble ferric hydroxide. Thus citric acid prevents the discolouration of the syrup from its normal green to a reddish brown tint. The peppermint spirit masks the taste of ferrous sulphate and improves the taste of the syrup.

3. What is the use of ferrous sulphate syrup?

   Answer: This is used to treat iron deficiency anaemia.

4. What patient guidance required while dispensing this syrup?

   Answer:

   - Measure the dose using the measuring spoon or devise supplied.
   - Dilute it with water before swallowing. This would prevent staining of teeth.
   - Take after meal to reduce gastric irritation.
   - Do not exceed the dose.
   - If you miss the dose, take as soon as you remember if within one hour. Do not double the dose.

CHAPTER - 4

Elixirs

Elixirs are clear, sweetened and flavoured alcoholic solutions for oral use. Both water soluble and alcohol soluble drugs can be formulated in the form of elixir. In addition to alcohol and water, other solvents like glycerine and propylene glycol can also be used.

Sucrose, sorbitol, glycerine, saccharin etc. are used as sweetening agent. Elixirs containing more than 10-12% alcohol do not need preservative. Alcohol content may be a problem for those who do not like to have it.

Experiment - 7

Piperazine Citrate Elixir BPC

Objective: To prepare and dispense 50 ml Piperazine Citrate Elixir.

Principle: Piperazine citrate is a water soluble substance and can be easily dissolved in water. The taste of the solution can be improved by adding peppermint spirit, glycerine and syrup. The preparation may be suitably coloured with addition of Green S and Tartrazine solution.

Formula

Ingredients	Master Formula	Working Formula
Piperazine citrate	187.5 g	$\frac{187.5\ g}{1000\ ml} \times 50\ ml = 9.37\ g$
Peppermint spirit	5 ml	$\frac{5\ ml}{1000\ ml} \times 50\ ml = 0.25\ ml$
Green S & Tartrazine solution	15 ml	$\frac{15\ ml}{1000\ ml} \times 50\ ml = 0.75\ ml$
Glycerol	100 ml	$\frac{100\ ml}{1000\ ml} \times 50\ ml = 5\ ml$
Syrup	500 ml	$\frac{500\ ml}{1000\ ml} \times 50\ ml = 25\ ml$
Purified water q.s.to	1000 ml	50 ml

Procedure: The required quantity of Piperazine citrate is dissolved in about 10 ml purified water. Peppermint spirit, green S and tartrazine solution, glycerol, and syrup are added. Finally sufficient purified water is added to produce the required 50 ml.

Storage: It should be stored in a well closed container in a cool place protected from light.

Category: Anthelminitic.

Dose: 5-15 ml for seven consecutive days for pinworms; Up to 30 ml as single dose for roundworms.

Questions and Answers:

1. What is the percentage of Piperazine citrate in the elixir?

   Answer: 18.75 % (w/v)

2. What are the uses of each ingredient of the product?

   Answer: Piperazine citrate is medicament; Peppermint spirit is flavouring agent; Green S and tartrazine solution is colouring agent; Glycerol and syrup are sweetening agent.

3. What is the use of Piperazine citrate elixir?

   Answer: Piperazine citrate elixir is used for the treatment of roundworm and pinworm. As it requires to be used at least for seven consecutive days, its popularity has decreased. Newer and better alternatives are available: mebendazole, albendazole and pyrantel.

4. What patient guidance is required while dispensing this elixir?

   Answer:

   - Take the medicine for seven days. Repeat after one week in serious infection.
   - Personal Hygiene: washing of hands and buttock after each motion, washing of night garments, under garments and bed linen daily till patient is free of worms.

Experiment - 8

Paediatric Paracetamol Elixir BPC

Objective: To prepare and dispense 50 ml Paediatric Paracetamol Elixir.

Principle: Paracetamol is not soluble to the extent in water to make a solution which would have one dose in 5 ml (120 mg / 5 ml). But it is readily soluble in alcohol, propylene glycol and glycerol. The mixture of these solvents serves as acceptable solvent for paracetamol. The solution is suitably preserved, flavoured and sweetened.

Formula

Ingredients	Master Formula	Working Formula
Paracetamol	24 g	$\frac{24\ g}{1000\ ml}\times 50\ ml = 1.2\ g$
Amaranth solution	2 ml	$\frac{2\ ml}{1000\ ml}\times 50\ ml = 0.1\ ml$
Chloroform spirit	20 ml	$\frac{20\ ml}{1000\ ml}\times 50\ ml = 1\ ml$
Concentrated raspberry juice	25 ml	$\frac{25\ ml}{1000\ ml}\times 50\ ml = 1.25\ ml$
Alcohol (95%)	100 ml	$\frac{100\ ml}{1000\ ml}\times 50\ ml = 5\ ml$
Propylene glycol	100 ml	$\frac{100\ ml}{1000\ ml}\times 50\ ml = 5\ ml$
Invert syrup	275 ml	$\frac{275\ ml}{1000\ ml}\times 50\ ml = 13.75\ ml$
Glycerol q. s. to	1000 ml	50 ml

Procedure: The required quantity of paracetamol is dissolved in a mixture of alcohol, propylene glycol and chloroform spirit. Concentrated raspberry juice is diluted with invert syrup. The diluted raspberry juice and amaranth solution are added. Finally sufficient glycerol is added to produce the required 50 ml. The mixture is thoroughly mixed.

Storage: It should be stored in a well closed container in a cool place.

Category: Analgesic and Antipyretic.

Dose: 2 to 5 ml at 4 - 6 hour interval.

Discussion: Aqueous paracetamol solution is not feasible due to solubility constraint. Alternative option is to prepare aqueous suspension. The suspension requires need of shaking the bottle before measuring each dose. This is often inconvenience leading to non-uniformity of dosage especially in children. Hence a combination of three solvents is used to dissolve paracetamol to make a solution which is suitably flavoured and sweetened.

Questions and Answers

1. What is the percentage of Paracetamol in the elixir?

   Answer: 2.4 % (w/v)

2. What are the uses of each ingredient of the product?

   Answer: Paracetamol is medicament; alcohol, propylene glycol and glycerol are solvents / vehicles; chloroform spirit is preservative (but chloroform no longer permissible in oral products); amaranth is colouring agent; raspberry juice and invert sugar are for flavouring and sweetening purpose.

3. What is the use of paediatric paracetamol elixir?

   Answer: This paediatric elixir is used for reduction of pain and lowering of fever in children.

4. What patient guidance is required while dispensing this elixir?

   Answer: The mother of the child is to be given the following instruction:

   - Measure the dose using the supplied spoon or device.
   - Do not increase the dose without doctor's advice.

Experiment - 9

Cascara Elixir BPC

Objective: To prepare 50 ml Cascara Elixir.

Principle: Liquid extract of cascara is prepared by percolation. Liquorice powder is added to powder of cascara before percolation. Liquorice extract obtained along with cascara serves as flavouring agent.

The two combined extract obtained by percolation is mixed with coriander oil, anise oil, saccharin, alcohol, glycerol and water to develop a pleasantly flavoured, sweetened and palatable preparation.

Formula:

Ingredients	Master Formula	Working Formula
Cascara, in coarse powder	1000 g	$\frac{1000\ g}{1000\ ml} \times 50\ ml = 50\ g$
Liquorice, unpeeled, in coarse powder	125 g	$\frac{125\ g}{1000\ ml} \times 50\ ml = 6.25\ g$
Light magnesium oxide	50 g	$\frac{50\ g}{1000\ ml} \times 50\ ml = 2.5\ g$
Coriander oil	0.15 ml	$\frac{0.15\ ml}{1000\ ml} \times 50\ ml = 0.0075\ ml$
Anise oil	0.2 ml	$\frac{0.2\ ml}{1000\ ml} \times 50\ ml = 0.01\ ml$
Alcohol (90%)	12.5 ml	$\frac{12.5\ ml}{1000\ ml} \times 50\ ml = 0.625\ ml$
Saccharin sodium	1 g	$\frac{1\ g}{1000\ ml} \times 50\ ml = 0.05\ g = 50\ mg$
Glycerol	300 ml	$\frac{300\ ml}{1000\ ml} \times 50\ ml = 15\ ml$
Water q. s. To	1000 ml	50 ml

Procedure: The required quantity of cascara, liquorice and light magnesium oxide are mixed and then moistened with about 63 ml boiling water, stirring thoroughly. The mixture is macerated for 24 hours in a well covered vessel. The macerated moistened mass is packed in moderately tightly in a percolator. Percolation is performed with boiling water until exhausted. The percolate is evaporated to about 33 ml on a water bath.

Saccharin sodium dissolved in 0.6 ml water; coriander oil and anise oil dissolved in alcohol; and saccharin and volatile oil solutions mixed with glycerol are mixed together.

Concentrated percolate is added and mixed. Finally sufficient water is added to produce the required 50 ml shaking thoroughly. The solution is kept as such for 12 hours and filtered.

Storage: It should be stored in a well closed container in a cool place.

Category: Laxative.

Dose: 2 to 5 ml.

Discussion: Cascara elixir cannot be extemporaneously prepared for use. It takes long time and hence, it is desirable to prepare this in advance and dispense as required.

Questions and Answers

1. What is the use of each ingredients mentioned in the formula of the elixir?

   Answer: Cascara powder is for preparing medicament extract; liquorice is for preparing flavour extract; anise and coriander oil are flavouring agents; saccharin and glycerol are for improving taste and imparting sweetness; magnesium oxide is for adsorbing some bitter principles; alcohol is for dissolving volatile oils for quick mixing with aqueous solvents.

2. What is the use of magnesium oxide during extraction process?

   Answer: Cascara contains many bitter principles which are very irritating. In order to partially avoid them, crude drug is mixed with magnesium oxide. Magnesium oxide neutralizes some of these bitter principles. The neutralized bitter principles are partially extracted.

3. What is the use of this elixir?

   Answer: This is used in the treatment of constipation. Cascara is no longer used because of safety issues. Overdose leads to intestinal pain and severe diarrhoea with electrolyte disbalance.

4. What patient guidance is required while dispensing this elixir?

   Answer: The mother of the child is to be given the following instruction:

   - Measure the dose using the supplied spoon or device.
   - Do not increase the dose without doctor's advice.

Experiment - 10

Terpin Hydrate Elixir IP 1966

Objective: To prepare and dispense 20 ml Terpin Hydrate Elixir

Principle: Terpin hydrate elixir is a sweetened hydroalcoholic solution of Terpin hydrate.

Formula:

Ingredients	Master Formula (for 1000 ml)	Working Formula (for 20 ml)
Terpin Hydrate	50 g	$\frac{50\ g}{1000\ ml} \times 20\ ml = 1\ g$
Orange Oil	0.2 ml	$\frac{0.2\ ml}{1000\ ml} \times 20\ ml = 0.004\ ml$ $(though\ less\ than\ 1\ drop\ is\ needed,$ $for\ convenience\ 1\ drop\ is\ to\ be\ used)$
Glycerin	400 ml	$\frac{400\ ml}{1000\ ml} \times 20\ ml = 8\ ml$
Alcohol	425 ml	$\frac{425\ ml}{1000\ ml} \times 20\ ml = 8.5\ ml$
Syrup	100 ml	$\frac{100\ ml}{1000\ ml} \times 20\ ml = 2\ ml$
Purified Water q. s. to	1000 ml	20 ml

Procedure: The required quantity of Terpin Hydrate is dissolved in alcohol. Successively orange oil, glycerine, and syrup are added and mixed. Finally, sufficient purified water is added and mixed to make the required volume.

Storage: Store in a well closed container in a cool place.

Category: Expectorant

Dose: 4 ml

Questions and Answers:

1. What are the uses of each component of Terpin Hydrate Elixir?
   Answer:
   - Terpin Hydrate – Medicament (expectorant)
   - Orange oil – Flavouring agent
   - Glycerine – Soothe the mucous and a cosolvent.
   - Alcohol – To solubilise Terpin Hydrate, Flavouring agent,
   - Syrup – Sweetened vehicle.
   - Water – Vehicle.
2. What is the use of Terpin Hydrate Elixir?

   Answer: It is used as expectorant in cough in chronic bronchitis.
3. What patient guidance is required while dispensing - Terpin Hydratc Elixir?

   Answer: Measure the dose using the supplied spoon.

CHAPTER - 5

Linctuses

The linctuses are viscous liquid preparations, sweetened with syrup, designed to soothe sore mucous membranes in the treatment of cough. The high proportion of syrup (also glycerine) has a demulcent effect on the membranes of the throat. The dose volume is kept at minimum, usually 5 ml and should be taken undiluted and slowly to prolong the demulcent action.

As they are viscous preparations, the complete transfer from the measure to the bottle is difficult. There would be significant volume on the inside of the measure despite of careful draining. Like suspensions and emulsions, the volume adjustment should be done in tared or calibrated bottle in which medicine is to be supplied. The linctuses should be labelled with "Sip and Swallow Slowly without Addition of water". They need to be measured using the supplied spoon to avoid inaccuracy of dose. The domestic measures' (spoons) capacity varies widely and hence it is recommended to use supplied measuring spoon or device.

They should be stored at constant temperature as temperature fluctuation may cause sucrose crystallization from the linctuses.

Experiment - 11

Simple Linctus BPC

Objective: To prepare and dispense 50 ml Simple Linctus.

Principle: The simple Linctus is a solution of citric acid in simple syrup to which flavouring agents are added.

Formula

<table>
<tr><th>Ingredients</th><th>Master Formula</th><th>Working Formula</th><th></th></tr>
<tr><td>Citric acid monohydrate</td><td>25 g</td><td>$\frac{25\text{ g}}{1000\text{ ml}} \times 50\text{ ml} = 1.25\text{ g}$</td><td rowspan="5">Note: Chloroform is no longer permitted in internal preparations and hence chloroform spirit is required to be omitted from the preparation. 0.1% Sodium Benzoate can be used as presser-vative.</td></tr>
<tr><td>Concentrated Anise Water</td><td>10 ml</td><td>$\frac{10\text{ ml}}{1000\text{ ml}} \times 50\text{ ml} = 0.5\text{ ml}$</td></tr>
<tr><td>Amaranth solution</td><td>15 ml</td><td>$\frac{15\text{ ml}}{1000\text{ ml}} \times 50\text{ ml} = 0.75\text{ ml}$</td></tr>
<tr><td>Chloroform spirit</td><td>60 ml</td><td>$\frac{60\text{ ml}}{1000\text{ ml}} \times 50\text{ ml} = 3\text{ ml}$</td></tr>
<tr><td>Syrup q. s. to</td><td>1000 ml</td><td>50 ml</td></tr>
</table>

Procedure: Chloroform spirit, concentrated anise water, and amaranth solution are mixed. The citric acid is dissolved in this mixture. Finally the volume is made up with sufficient syrup.

Storage: It should be stored in a well closed container in a cool place avoiding marked fluctuation in temperature.

Category: Demulcent.

Dose: 5 ml three times daily.

Questions and Answers

1. What are the uses of each ingredients of the formula?

   Answer: Syrup serves as vehicle; Citric acid is the medicament; concentrated anise water and chloroform spirit are flavouring agents; and amaranth is used as colouring agent.

2. What is the use of simple Linctus?

   Answer: This is useful as demulcent in soothing irritating throat in the treatment of cough. This is also used to prepare Paediatric Simple Linctus.

3. What patient guidance is required while dispensing Simple Linctus to the patients?

   Answer:

   - Do not swallow with water.
   - Sip and swallow slowly undiluted.

Experiment - 12

Paediatric Simple Linctus BPC

Objective: To prepare and dispense 50 ml Paediatric Simple Linctus.

Principle: The Paediatric Simple Linctus is a solution of citric acid in simple syrup to which flavouring agents are added. This can be prepared by diluting Simple Linctus with simple syrup to contain 1.25 ml per 5 ml of the product.

Formula

Ingredients	Master Formula	Working Formula
Simple Linctus	250 ml	$\frac{250\text{ ml}}{1000\text{ ml}} \times 50\text{ ml} = 12.5\text{ ml}$
Syrup q. s. to	1000 ml	50 ml

Procedure: The required quantity of Simple Linctus is diluted to 50 ml in a calibrated bottle with syrup (simple syrup).

Storage: It should be stored in a well closed container in a cool place avoiding marked fluctuation in temperature.

Category: Demulcent.

Dose: 1 to 5 year child: 5 ml up to four times a day.
6 to 12 year child: 10 ml up to four times a day.

Questions and Answers

1. What is the use of Paediatric Simple Linctus?

   Answer: It is demulcent. It coats the irritating throat and provides symptomatic relief of cough.

2. What patient guidance is required while dispensing Paediatric Simple Linctus to the patients?

   Answer: The mother is instructed:

   - Measure the dose with the supplied spoon or measuring device.
   - Tell the child to sip and swallow slowly without water.
   - Keep all medicines out of reach of children.
   - Consult your doctor if the symptoms of the child remain even after 5 days.

CHAPTER - 6

Solutions

Solutions are liquid preparations containing one or more dissolved medicinal ingredients. Depending upon the dissolved substance(s) and the type of the solvent(s), the solutions can be used for a variety of purposes like for oral use, ophthalmic use, nasal use, or external use. However, the solutions do have different nomenclatures too and such nomenclatures are based on composition of solutions like Syrups (containing sugars), Elixirs (containing hydroalcoholic solvent), Tinctures (containing active ingredients obtained by extraction from crude drugs) etc.

The solutions are prepared by dissolving the drug substances (Aqueous Iodine Solution) or by chemical reaction (strong Solution of Ammonium Acetate).

Experiment - 13

Aqueous Iodine Solution IP [1966] [Synonym: Lugol's Solution]

Objective: To prepare and dispense 50 ml of Aqueous Iodine Solution.

Principle: Iodine is not soluble in water. In order to dissolve Iodine in water, Potassium Iodide is included in the formula. Iodine and Potassium Iodide reacts to form Potassium tri-iodide and this tri-iodide is soluble.

$$I_2 + KI \rightleftharpoons KI_3$$

Formula

Ingredients	Master Formula	Working Formula
Iodine	50 g	$\frac{50\ g}{1000\ ml} \times 50\ ml = 2.5\ g$
Potassium Iodide	100 g	$\frac{100\ g}{1000\ ml} \times 50\ ml = 5\ g$
Purified Water q.s. to	1000 ml	50 ml

Procedure: The required quantity of Potassium Iodide and Iodine are dissolved in around 10 ml purified water in a glass measuring cylinder. The sufficient purified water is then added to make up the volume to 50 ml. [Do not use metal spatula to handle Iodine and protect the balance pan using a weighing paper].

Storage: It should be stored in a well closed iodine resistant container.

Category: Source of Iodine.

Dose: 0.3 to 1 ml.

Discussion: Aqueous Iodine Solution is a transparent liquid having deep brown colour and odour of Iodine. The solubility of Iodine in water is just 1 in 3000 (0.03%). The addition of Potassium or Sodium Iodide increased the solubility through formation of water soluble complex.

The strength of the solution should be expressed as Iodine – 5% and the total Iodine – 13%. The preparation is meant for treatment of hypothyroidism, a condition known as goitre. The preparation can also be used as antiseptic but after dilution with water.

Questions and Answers

1. What is the percentage of Iodine in this Aqueous Iodine Solution?

   Answer: 5% Iodine and Total Iodine – 13%.

2. What is the purpose of Potassium Iodide in this preparation?

   Answer: At this strength (5%), Iodine is not soluble in water. Potassium Iodide is added to covert Iodine into tri-iodide form through a reversible reaction which is soluble.

3. Why are Iodine and Potassium Iodide dissolved first in small amount of water and then diluted to the required volume?

   Answer: Iodine with Potassium Iodide forms poly-iodides. Higher poly-iodides are more soluble than lower ones. Higher iodides are formed in concentrated solution. Hence, the solution is first prepared in small amount of solvent to make concentrated solution to get rapid solution. This solution is then diluted to required volume.

4. Why metal spatulas are not used handling Iodine?

   Answer: Iodine reacts with Iron [$Fe + I_2 \rightarrow FeI_2$]. Iron oxidizes. Plastics too have problems. Glass and earthenware are appropriate.

5. What is the use of this preparation and what guidance you would provide to the patient?

   Answer: This preparation can be used in thyrotoxicosis and thyrotoxic crisis (pre-operative treatment of hyperthyroidism).

   This is also used to supply iodine in iodine deficiency conditions. The iodine deficiency causes endemic goiter and results in deaf mutism, intellectual deficit, spasticity, impaired mental function. Now a days, salt iodization (consumption of iodized salts) is used to redress the issue of iodine deficiency.

   The patient should be advised to dilute well with milk or water before swallowing.

   The solution can also be used to disinfect drinking water in emergency.

   When used as antiseptic:

   - Application on intact skin: Dilute with equal volume of water and apply the solution to the washed / cleaned intact skin several minutes before the operation.

- Application on wounds: Dilute with equal volume of water and apply the solution to the thoroughly cleaned wound with a sterile dressing. Iodine treated skin should not be covered with tight or occlusive bandages. This may cause irritation and blistering of the skin.

Experiment - 14

Strong Iodine Solution IP [1966]

Objective: To prepare and dispense 50 ml of Strong Iodine Solution.

Principle: Iodine is not soluble in water, but is soluble in alcohol. The Iodine reacts with alcohol and the resultant Ethyl Iodide has no antimicrobial effect. This reaction is to be prevented. The potassium tri-iodide does not react with alcohol. In order to dissolve Iodine in water, Potassium Iodide is included in the formula. Iodine and Potassium Iodide reacts to form Potassium tri-iodide and this tri-iodide is soluble in water and alcohol.

$$I_2 + KI \rightleftharpoons KI_3$$

Formula

Ingredients	Master Formula	Working Formula
Iodine	100 g	$\frac{100\text{ g}}{1000\text{ ml}} \times 50\text{ ml} = 5\text{ g}$
Potassium Iodide	60 g	$\frac{60\text{ g}}{1000\text{ ml}} \times 50\text{ ml} = 3\text{ g}$
Purified Water	100 ml	5 ml
Alcohol (90%) q.s. to	1000 ml	50 ml

Procedure: The required quantity of Potassium Iodide and Iodine are dissolved in purified water in a glass measuring cylinder. Sufficient alcohol (90%) is then added to make up the volume to 50 ml. [Do not use metal spatula to handle Iodine and protect the balance pan using a weighing paper].

Storage: It should be stored in a well closed iodine resistant container [well closed container to prevent loss of alcohol].

Category: Antiseptic.

Discussion: Strong Iodine Solution is a alcoholic iodine solution containing 10% Iodine and 6% Potassium Iodide. The preparation can be used as antiseptic after suitable dilution with water.

Questions and Answers

1. What is the percentage of Iodine in this Aqueous Iodine Solution?

   Answer: 10% Iodine.

2. What is the purpose of Potassium Iodide in this preparation when Iodine is soluble in alcohol at this concentration?

   Answer: At this strength (10%), Iodine is not soluble in water, but is soluble in alcohol (90%). If we dissolve Iodine in alcohol, there would be reaction between Iodine and Ethyl Alcohol forming Ethyl Iodide. This Ethyl Iodide has no antimicrobial activity. As Potassium tri-Iodide does not react with Ethyl Alcohol, Potassium Iodide is added to covert Iodine into tri-iodide. With this antimicrobial activity (antiseptic) is retained. Addition of Potassium Iodide prevents the formation of Ethyl Iodide. Iodides are devoid of antiseptic activity but they convert back to Iodine which is effective.

   Besides, as the product is available as solution of tri-iodide, they can be easily diluted which would have not been possible if Iodine just dissolved in alcohol.

3. Why is alcohol used as solvent?

   Answer: Alcohol is used as solvent because it helps in penetration and absorption of Iodine as it dissolves percutaneous fat. In addition, it is also antiseptic.

4. Why metal spatulas are not used handling Iodine?

   Answer: Iodine reacts with Iron [$Fe + I_2 \rightarrow FeI_2$]. Iron oxidizes. Plastics too have problems. Glass and earthenware are appropriate.

5. What is the use of Strong Iodine Solution?

   Answer: It is used as antiseptic for application on the skin prior to surgery. Now PVP-Iodine preparations are preferred.

Experiment - 15

Weak Iodine Solution IP [1966] [Synonym: Iodine Tincture]

Objective: To prepare and dispense 50 ml of Weak Iodine Solution.

Principle: Iodine is not soluble in water, but is soluble in alcohol. The Iodine reacts with alcohol and the resultant Ethyl Iodide has no antimicrobial effect. This reaction is to be prevented. The potassium tri-iodide does not react with alcohol. In order to dissolve Iodine in water, Potassium Iodide is included in the formula. Iodine and Potassium Iodide reacts to form Potassium tri-iodide and this tri-iodide is soluble in water and alcohol.

$$I_2 + KI \rightleftharpoons KI_3$$

Formula

Ingredients	Master Formula	Working Formula
Iodine	20 g	$\frac{20\text{ g}}{1000\text{ ml}} \times 50\text{ ml} = 1\text{ g}$
Potassium Iodide	25 g	$\frac{25\text{ g}}{1000\text{ ml}} \times 50\text{ ml} = 1.25\text{ g}$
Alcohol (50%) q.s. to	1000 ml	50 ml

Procedure: The required quantity of Potassium Iodide and Iodine are dissolved in around 5 ml purified water in a glass measuring cylinder/mortar. Sufficient alcohol (50%) is then added to make up the volume to 50 ml. [Do not use metal spatula to handle Iodine and protect the balance pan using a weighing paper].

Storage: It should be stored in a well closed iodine resistant container [tight container to prevent loss of alcohol].

Category: Antiseptic.

Discussion: Weak Iodine Solution is hydro-alcoholic iodine solution containing 2% Iodine and 2.5% Potassium Iodide. The preparation can be used as antiseptic after suitable dilution with water.

Questions and Answers

1. What is the percentage of Iodine in Weak Iodine Solution?

   Answer: 2% Iodine.

2. What is the purpose of Potassium Iodide in this preparation when Iodine is soluble in alcohol at this concentration?

   Answer: At this strength (2%), Iodine is not soluble in water, but is soluble in alcohol (50%). If we dissolve Iodine in alcohol, there would be reaction between Iodine and Ethyl Alcohol forming Ethyl Iodide. This Ethyl Iodide has no antimicrobial activity. As Potassium tri-Iodide does not react with Ethyl Alcohol, Potassium Iodide is added to covert Iodine into tri-iodide. With this antimicrobial activity (antiseptic) is retained. Addition of Potassium Iodide prevents the formation of Ethyl Iodide. Iodides are devoid of antiseptic activity but they convert back to Iodine which is effective.

   Besides, as the product is available as solution of tri-iodide, they can be easily diluted which would have not been possible if Iodine just dissolved in alcohol.

3. Why metal spatulas are not used handling Iodine?

   Answer: Iodine reacts with Iron [$Fe + I_2 \rightarrow FeI_2$]. Iron oxidizes. Plastics too have problems. Glass and earthenware are appropriate.

4. What is the use of Weak Iodine Solution?

   Answer: This is a good antiseptic applied topically to the skin as first aid. The reddish brown colour is produced over the applied part indicating the application part. Due to its alcohol content, it is irritating to use in open wounds.

   Alcohol being solvent provides additional antibacterial action and improves penetration (and absorption) of Iodine (dissolving fats).

   When used as antiseptic:

   - Application on intact skin: Apply the solution to the washed / cleaned intact skin several minutes before the operation.
   - Application on wounds: Apply the solution to the thoroughly cleaned wound with a sterile dressing. Iodine treated skin should not be covered with tight or occlusive bandages. This may cause irritation and blistering of the skin.

     [Two different approaches are followed in disinfecting intact skin and wounds. In the former, the rapid action is important and irritation has no meaning. But the latter requires a more tolerable preparation. Hence, aqueous solution is preferred for wound disinfection and hydro-alcoholic solution (Tincture) is preferred for intact skin.

At present a better Iodine product: Povidone – Iodine is available for use.

Experiment - 16

Cresol with Soap Solution IP [1966] [Synonym: Lysol]

Objective: To prepare 50 ml of Cresol with Soap Solution.

Principle: Cresol has very low solubility in water, just 2%. *In situ* prepared soap is used to solubilize large amount cresol in water. The soap is prepared by interacting fatty acids of vegetable oil and potassium hydroxide.

Formula

Ingredients	Master Formula	Working Formula
Cresol	500 ml	$\frac{500\ \text{ml}}{1000\ \text{ml}} \times 50\ \text{ml} = 25\ \text{ml}$
Vegetable oil	180 g	$\frac{180\ \text{g}}{1000\ \text{ml}} \times 50\ \text{ml} = 9\ \text{g}$; This is equal to 10 ml assuming the density of oil as 0.9 g/ml.
Potassium hydroxide	42 g	$\frac{42\ \text{g}}{1000\ \text{ml}} \times 50\ \text{ml} = 2.1\ \text{g}$
Purified Water q.s. to	1000 ml	50 ml

Procedure: Potassium hydroxide is dissolved in around 12 ml purified water in glass beaker. The vegetable oil is added. The mixture is heated on a water bath with mixing. Heating is continued until the saponification is complete. [The saponification can be ascertained by adding few drops of mixture to water. No separation of oily drops is indicative of complete saponification]. Then Cresol is added and mixed thoroughly. Finally purified water is added to make the required volume.

Storage: It should be stored in a well closed container protected from light.

Category: Disinfectant.

Discussion: Cresol with soap solution contains 50% (v/v) of cresol. It is prepared by dissolving cresol in *in situ* prepared soap solution. The vegetable oil like cotton seed, linseed or soybean oils may be used for making the soap. Coconut and palm kernel oils cannot be used. Prolonged heating is often necessary to effect saponification if the above method is used. The process of saponification can be accelerated / hastened by:

- Replacing part of the vegetable oil with oleic acid. Oleic acid reacts immediately with alkali (potassium hydroxide) forming soap. This soap accelerates the saponification on heating; or
- Adding small amount of industrial methylated spirit to the oil – alkali mixture and heating in a closed vessel until saponification is complete. The alcohol is finally removed by further heating in an open vessel.

  Cresol with soap solution is used as general disinfectant at the following dilution:

  for drains, 1 in 20;

  for heavily infected linens, 1 in 40;

  for floors and walls, 1 in 100.

Questions and Answers

1. What is the strength of cresol in cresol with soap solution?

   Answer: 50% v/v.

2. What is the need of a solubilised product of cresol? Can we directly use cresol instead?

   Answer: The solubilised product is easily dispersible. Soap helps in ready dispersion throughout the system like drain to which it is added. This also assists penetration into greasy or coagulated materials.

   If cresol is added directly, it would not be effective as it cannot get dispersed.

3. Can this be used as antiseptic for application over the skin?

   Answer: It cannot be used on skin due to its corrosive action on living tissues. But similar solubilised products: Chloroxylenol solution can be sued as antiseptic for application on living tissues.

Experiment - 17

Strong Ammonium Acetate Solution IP [1966] [Synonym: Liquor Ammoni Acetatis Fortis]

Objective: To prepare 50 ml of Strong Ammonium Acetate Solution.

Principle: Ammonium Acetate is produced by mixing Glacial Acetic Acid and Sodium Bicarbonate. But the reaction is not complete and acetic acid is incompletely neutralised. Strong Ammonia is added to carefully to make the solution almost neutral.

$$CH_3COOH + NH_4HCO_3 = CH_3COONH_4 + H_2O + CO_2$$

$$CH_3COOH + NH_4OH = CH_3COONH_4 + H_2O$$

Formula

Ingredients	Master Formula	Working Formula
Glacial Acetic Acid	453 g	$\frac{453\ g}{1000\ ml} \times 50\ ml = 22.65\ g$; This is equal to 21.63 ml [the specific gravity of glacial acetic acid = 1.047].
Ammonium Bicarbonate	470 g	$\frac{470\ g}{1000\ ml} \times 50\ ml = 23.5\ g$
Ammonia Solution, Strong	100 ml or qs	$\frac{100\ g}{1000\ ml} \times 50\ ml = 5$ ml or qs
Purified Water q.s. to	1000 ml	50 ml

Procedure: Glacial Acetic Acid is mixed with about 17 ml purified water. Ammonium Bicarbonate is added in small quantity at a time to Glacial Acetic Acid – Water mixture until it is all dissolved. Sufficient Ammonia solution is added slowly until one drop of the resulting solution diluted with ten drops water gives a full Blue colour with one drop of solution of Bromothymol Blue and full Yellow colour with one drop of Thymol blue. Then sufficient purified water is added to produce the required volume (50 ml).

Storage: It should be stored in a lead free glass bottle.

Category: Diaphoretic [a substance that promotes sweating].

Dose: 1 to 4 ml

Discussion: Strong Ammonium Acetate is a thin syrupy liquid with an odour of ammonia and acetic acid. The reaction for formation of Ammonium Acetate (Acetic Acid + Sodium Bicarbonate) should be carried out in a large open vessel to allow easy escape of carbon dioxide. This would also avoid spillage due to frothing.

The use of two indicators ensures the pH range of the product: 7.6 to 8.0.

	pH range	Colour
Bromothymol Blue	6.1 to 7.6	Yellow to Blue
Thymol Blue	8.0 to 9.6	Yellow to Blue

The smell of the product is also a useful indicator: Odour of acetic acid becomes less perceivable towards the end point.

The Ammonia solution is to be added very carefully; otherwise the pH of the product may exceed 8.0. Care should be taken not to contaminate the product with indicators.

Questions and Answers

1. What is the strength of Ammonium Acetate in this product?

   Answer: 57.50% w/v.

2. Why the lead free bottles are used for storage of Strong Ammonium Acetate Solution?

   Answer: Ammonium Acetate dissolves salts easily. Lead salts are toxic.

3. What is the use of two indicators?

   Answer: The two indicators: Bromothymol Blue and Thymol Blue are used to ensure physiologically compatible pH of the product (pH 7.6 to 8.0).

4. What is the use of this Strong Solution of Ammonium Acetate?

   Answer: This is used as mild expectorant, diaphoretic and diuretic at a dose of 1 to 5 ml.

5. How is dilute solution of ammonium acetate solution prepared? What is its use?

   Answer: The dilute solution of ammonium acetate is also known as ammonium acetate solution. This can be prepared by diluting strong solution of ammonium acetate to 8 times its volume with freshly boiled and cooled water [1 ml is to be diluted to 8 ml]. This dilute ammonium acetate solution has similar activities as the strong solution but the dose is 8 to 40 ml.

Experiment - 18

Strong Solution of Ferric Chloride BPC (1977)

Objective: To prepare 50 ml of Strong Solution of Ferric Chloride.

Principle: Solution of Ferric Chloride is prepared by dissolving iron in hydrochloric acid and oxidizing this resulting solution of ferrous chloride with Nitric acid as oxidizing agent.

Formula

Ingredients	Master Formula	Working Formula
Iron	210 g	$\frac{210\text{ g}}{1050\text{ ml}} \times 50\text{ ml} = 10\text{ g}$
Concentrated Nitric Acid	90 ml	$\frac{90\text{ ml}}{1050\text{ ml}} \times 50\text{ ml} = 4.3\text{ ml}$
Concentrated Hydrochloric Acid	1230 ml	$\frac{1230\text{ ml}}{1050\text{ ml}} \times 50\text{ ml} = 59\text{ ml}$
Purified Water q. s. to approx.	1050 ml	50 ml

Procedure: The required quantity of iron is taken in a flask. A mixture 35 ml of hydrochloric acid and 20 ml water is added and gently heated until effervescence ceases. This is then boiled and filtered to separate un-dissolved iron. The flask is washed with little water and washing is passed through the filter.

20 ml of hydrochloric acid is added to the combined filtrate and washing and mixed. The solution is then slowly poured into nitric acid. It is gently warmed to promote chemical reaction. The product is evaporated until precipitation begins to form 3 ml hydrochloric acid is added. Finally volume is adjusted to 50 ml. (or the quantity which would have density of 1.42 to 1.46 g/ml).

Storage: It should be stored in a well closed container.

Category: Haematinic (but not used as such, it is used to make Ferric Chloride Solution which can be used medicinally as haematinic).

Discussion: The following reactions take place while preparing the Ferric Chloride solution:

$$Fe + 2\ HCL \rightarrow FeCl_2 + H_2$$

The un-dissolved iron and iron carbide impurities are removed by filtration.

$$2FeCl_2 + Cl_2 \rightarrow 2FeCl_3$$

$$2HNO_3 = H_2O + N_2O_5;\ N_2O_5 = 2NO + 3O;$$
$$6HCl + 3O = 3H_2O + 3Cl_2$$

$$6FeCl_2 + 3Cl_2 = 6FeCl_3$$

The combined reactions can be written as:

$$3FeCl_2 + 3HCl + HNO_3 = 3FeCl_3 + 2H_2O + NO$$

Questions and Answers

1. Why is Nitric acid chosen as oxidizing agent?

   Answer: The reduction products with nitric acid are volatile and can easily be removed by boiling. This would have pure product.

2. What is the need of additional Hydrochloric acid when reaction is already completed?

   Answer: After the reaction with nitric acid, the solution is evaporated till precipitation commences. The appearance of precipitation is an indication of formation of Ferric Oxychloride due to hydrolysis. The commencement of this reaction is an indication of achievement of the concentration. The evaporation needs to be stopped at this stage.

   $$FeCl_3 + H_2O = Fe(OH)Cl_2 + HCl$$

   The already formed Ferric Oxychloride is dissolved by adding hydrochloric acid. This is a backward reaction.

3. What is the use of Strong Ferric Chloride Solution?

   Answer: Strong Ferric Chloride Solution is as such not used medicinally. This is used to make ferric chloride solution which can be used as haematinic at a dose of 0.3 to 1 ml. Ferric chloride solution can be prepared by diluting strong ferric chloride solution with purified water.

   Formula: Strong Ferric Chloride Solution – 250 ml and Purified water to make 1000 ml.

   Due to availability of better iron preparations like various forms of ferrous sulphate, ferric chloride is no longer used medicinally.

CHAPTER - 7

Suspensions for Oral Use

Oral suspensions are used when the medicament(s) are not soluble in queous vehicle. Purified water is the vehicle of choice. The oral liquid preparations have several advantages: easy administration, quicker action compared to solid dosage forms. However, they need to be measured using the supplied spoon to avoid inaccuracy of dose. The domestic measures' (spoons) capacity varies widely and hence it is recommended to use supplied measuring spoon or device. For oral suspensions. the bottles need to be shaken before measuring the dose.

Experiment - 19

Magnesium Hydroxide Mixture BP

Objective: To prepare and dispense 50 ml Magnesium Hydroxide Mixture.

Principle: Magnesium hydroxide mixture is a suspension of magnesium hydroxide in water. Magnesium hydroxide, the medicament, is prepared by the two chemical reactions:

$$MgSO_4, 7\ H_2O + 2\ NaOH \rightarrow Mg(OH)_2 + Na_2SO_4 + 7\ H_2O$$ [precipitation reaction]

$$MgO + H_2O \rightarrow Mg(OH)_2$$ [hydration reaction]

The reaction by product, Sodium Sulphate, is to be removed through several washings.

Formula

Ingredients	Master Formula	Working Formula	Note: 0.1 % Sodium Benzoate can be used as preservative. Chloroform is to be removed.
Magnesium sulphate	47.5 g	$\frac{47.5\ g}{1000\ ml} \times 50\ ml = 2.4\ g$	
Sodium hydroxide	15 g	$\frac{15\ g}{1000\ ml} \times 50\ ml = 0.75\ g = 750\ mg$	
Light magnesium oxide	52.5 g	$\frac{52.5\ g}{1000\ ml} \times 50\ ml = 2.6\ g$	
Chloroform	2.5 ml	$\frac{2.5\ g}{1000\ ml} \times 50\ ml = 0.13\ ml$	
Citric acid	1 g	$\frac{1\ g}{1000\ ml} \times 50\ ml = 0.05\ g = 50\ mg$	
Purified water q.s. to	1000 ml	50 ml	

Procedure: The required quantity of sodium hydroxide is dissolved in 8 ml of purified water. Light magnesium oxide is triturated in a mortar with the sodium hydroxide solution to form a smooth cream. This suspension is diluted to about 13 ml.

The above suspension is poured in a thin stream into a solution of magnesium sulphate in 13 ml purified water (beaker) with stirring continuously during mixing.

The precipitate formed is allowed to settle and the clear liquid is removed. The residue is transferred to a calico strainer and washed thoroughly with water to remove sulphate.

The washed precipitate is mixed with purified water and then chloroform and citric acid are dissolved in it.

Finally sufficient purified water is added to make 50 ml.

[The transfer of the suspension from the measuring cylinder to the container is not easy. Complete transfer is not possible. Hence the adjustment of volume is advisable in calibrated bottle in which the product is to be supplied].

Storage: It should be stored in a well closed container in a cool place, but not to be kept in refrigerator.

Category: Antacid and Laxative.

Dose: Antacid – 5 to 10 ml and Laxative – 15 to 30 ml.

Discussion: Magnesium hydroxide mixture is prepared by combination of two reactions: precipitation and hydration. If prepared entirely by hydration, the product would become viscous and unpourable on keeping. On the other hand, if prepared entirely on precipitation, the sediments settle quickly. Mixture prepared by combination reactions are not excessively thick and do not separate quickly.

Citric acid minimizes the action of alkaline product in soda lime glass. It also improves the taste of the product. Earlier it was recommended to store magnesium hydroxide mixture in lead and arsenic free glass bottles. The blue coloured bottles were designated as arsenic free. Now all medicinal glass bottles are free from heavy metals.

Chloroform is preservative. But the use of chloroform in internal products is not permissible now. Methyl baraben (0.2 %) or sodium benzoate (0.125%) may be added as preservative.

The flavouring agent like volatile oil may be added to improve the taste.

The magnesium hydroxide mixture is also known as milk of magnesia.

Questions and Answers

1. What are the uses of each ingredients of the formula?

   Answer: Magnesium sulphate, sodium hydroxide and magnesium oxide are included in the formula to produce the medicament, magnesium hydroxide. Chloroform is preservative (now not permissible) and citric acid minimises the action of alkali on glass.

2. What are the uses of magnesium hydroxide mixture?

   Answer: Magnesium hydroxide mixture is used as gastric antacid to treat hyperacidity or heart burn and as laxative to treat constipation. However, when used in chronic hyperacidity (long term use) as antacid, a combination product with calcium or aluminium antacid is advisable. The combination overcomes the laxative effects of magnesium hydroxide. Phosphate supplementation is also necessary as absorption of dietary phosphates is prevented by polyvalent metallic ions by forming insoluble salt/complex.

3. How do you test that the product is free from sulphate?

   Answer: The presence of sodium sulphate may cause crimping action in the stomach. Hence the sulphate is removed by washing. The presence/absence of sulphate can be tested by adding barium chloride solution to the supernatant or washed water. The appearance of white colour is an indication of presence of sulphate which needs further washing.

4. What patient guidance is required while dispensing this magnesium hydroxide mixture to patients?

   Answer:

   - Shake well before use.
   - Measure the dose using supplied spoon or measuring devise.
   - Store in a cool place but not in refrigerator. [Keeping in refrigerator would increase the size of dispersed particles leading to stability issue and different in taste].

Experiment - 20

Aluminium Hydroxide Gel (Aluminium Hydroxide Mixture)

Objective: To prepare and dispense 50 ml Aluminium Hydroxide Gel B.P.

Principle: Aluminium Hydroxide Gel is an aqueous suspension of hydrated aluminium oxide together with varying quantities of aluminium carbonate. Aluminium Hydroxide is prepared by a chemical reaction between aluminium salt (Aluminium Sulphate or Potash Alum) and Alkaline Carbonate (Sodium Carbonate).

Formula:

Ingredients	Master Formula (for 1000 ml)	Working Formula (for 50 ml)
Aluminium Sulphate	355.6 g	$\frac{355.6\ g}{1000\ ml} \times 50\ ml = 17.78\ g$
Sodium Carbonate	336. 6 g	$\frac{336.6\ g}{1000\ ml} \times 50\ ml = 16.83\ g$
Peppermint Oil	2 ml	$\frac{2\ ml}{1000\ ml} \times 50\ ml = 0.1\ ml$
Sodium Benzoate	1 g	$\frac{1\ g}{1000\ ml} \times 50\ ml = 0.05\ g = 50\ mg$
Glycerine	50 ml	$\frac{50\ ml}{1000\ ml} \times 50\ ml = 2.5\ ml$
Purified Water q. s. to	1000 ml	50 ml

Procedure: Aluminium Sulphate is dissolved in water and heated. The hot solution is added with stirring to a hot solution of Sodium Carbonate. The gelatinous precipitate is washed to make it free of sulphate and sodium. (The wash water should be hot but not boiling, because precipitates redissolve in boiling water). The other ingredients are added. Finally, volume is adjusted. [It is difficult to completely transfer the quantity from a measuring device. It is preferable to adjust the volume in a calibrated bottle.]

Storage: Store in a cool place (do not freeze).

Category: Gastric antacid

Dose: 5 to 15 ml.

Discussion: As the medicament is prepared by chemical reaction, the precipitate is washed with hot water to make it free of sulphate and sodium. Boiling water (for washing) should be avoided as precipitate may redissolve.
The order of mixing is important. If it is reversed, alkali sulphate is trapped in the precipitate and is difficult to remove by washing.

Questions and Answers:

1. What are the uses of each component of Aluminium Hydroxide Gel?
   Answer:
   - Aluminium Sulphate and Sodium Carbonate are reactants for producing aluminium hydroxide.
   - Peppermint oil is flavouring agent.
   - Sodium Benzoate is preservative.
   - Glycerine is sweetening agent.
2. What is the use of Aluminium Hydroxide Gel?
   Answer: It is used as gastric antacid in the treatment of gastric ulcer. It provides a protective coating to the inflamed and ulcerated areas.
3. What patient guidance is required while dispensing Aluminium Hydroxide Gel?
   Answer:
   - Maintain different timing for medicines if two or more medicines are to be taken at the same time. Some medicines' absorption may be impaired by this medicine.
   - Shake well before use.
   - Do not keep in refrigerator.

CHAPTER - 8

Gargles, Mouth Washes and Paints

Gargles are aqueous solutions used in the prevention and treatment of throat infections. They are usually used after dilution with warm water. They are intended to bring the medicament into contact with mucous surface of throat. They are usually not meant for swallowing.

Mouth washes are similar to gargles but are intended to wash out the mouth. They are meant to improve oral hygiene and treat infection of the mouth.

Paints are liquid preparations intended for application to the skin or mucous membrane. Throat paints are viscous designed to have prolonged contact with the throat. Skin paints may have volatile solvent and on application solvent evaporates leaving a dry resinous film of medicament.

Experiment - 21

PVP - Iodine Gargle

Objective: To prepare and dispense 100 ml PVP – Iodine Gargle.

Principle: PVP – Iodine is soluble in water and 1 % w/v solution is prepared by dissolving in water.

Formula

Ingredients	Master Formula (for 1000 ml)	Working Formula (for 100 ml)
PVP - Iodine	10 g	$\frac{10\ g}{1000\ ml} \times 100\ ml = 1\ g$
Purified Water q. s. to	1000 ml	100 ml

Procedure: PVP – Iodine is dissolved in 90 ml purified water. Then volume is adjusted to 100 ml using purified water.

Storage: Store in a cool place.

Category: Antiseptic.

Discussion: PVP – Iodine is a chemical complex. It maintains an equilibrium state in an aqueous solution and releases free Iodine as free Iodine concentration decreases. Free Iodine acts as microbicidal agent.

Questions and Answers:

1. What are the uses of each component of PVP – Iodine Gargle?
   Answer:
   - PVP – Iodine is the active ingredient (source of Iodine); and
   - Purified Water – Vehicle (solvent).
2. What is the use of PVP-Iodine Gargle?

   Answer: It is used for the treatment of acute infections of the lining of the mouth and throat. It is also used as mouth wash.
3. What patient guidance is required while dispensing PVP – Iodine Gargle?
   Answer:
   - Gargle for 3 to 4 times a day.

- Do not swallow.
- Keep out of reach of children.

Experiment - 22

Chlorhexidine Mouthwash

Objective: To prepare and dispense 50 ml Chlorhexidine Mouthwash

Principle: Chlorhexidine Mouthwash is 0.2 % aqueous solution of chlorhexidine gluconate containing 7 % v/v alcohol (95 %).

Formula

Ingredients	Master Formula (for 100 ml)	Working Formula (for 50 ml)
Chlorhexidine Gluconate	0.2 g	$\frac{0.2\,g}{100\,ml} \times 50\,ml = 0.1\,g = 100\,mg$
Alcohol (95 % v/v)	7 ml	$\frac{7\,ml}{100\,ml} \times 50\,ml = 3.5\,ml$
Colouring agent	Qs	Qs
Flavoring agent	Qs	Qs
Purified Water q. s. to	100 ml	50 ml

Procedure: The required quantity of all ingredients is dissolved in water to make the required volume.

Storage: Sore in a cool dry place.

Category: Antiseptic

Discussion: The fabric which has been in contact with this mouthwash may stain if washed in solution containing hypochlorite.

Questions and Answers:

1. What are the uses of each component of Chlorhexidine Mouthwash?
   Answer: Chlorhexidine Gluconate is the medicament (antiseptic). Alcohol is also antiseptic. Purified water is the vehicle.
2. What is the use of Chlorhexidine Mouthwash?

   Answer: It is used to treat gingivitis (swelling, redness, bleeding gums).

3. What patient guidance is required while dispensing - Chlorhexidine Mouthwash?

   Answer:

   - Use to rinse mouth 3 or 4 times daily.
   - Avoid swallowing.

Experiment - 23

Compound Iodine Paint [Mandl's Paint]

Objective: To prepare and dispense 15 ml Compound Iodine Paint.

Principle: Compound Iodine Paint is a viscous Iodine solution. As it is difficult to completely transfer a viscous solution from the measuring jar/cylinder to the dispensing bottle, it is preferable to prepare little extra. Iodine is dissolved in presence of Potassium iodide. Iodine reacts with Potassium Iodide to form Potassium Triiodide. Triiodide is freely soluble. Glycerine is included as viscous vehicle. The preparation is slightly flavoured with Peppermint Oil and Alcohol is included to dissolve Peppermint Oil.

Formula

Ingredients	**Master Formula (for 1000 ml)**	**Working Formula (for 20 ml)**
Potassium Iodide	25 g	$\frac{25\,g}{1000\,ml} \times 20\,ml = 0.5\,g = 500\,mg$
Iodine	12.5 g	$\frac{12.5\,g}{1000\,ml} \times 20\,ml = 0.25\,g = 250\,mg$
Alcohol (90 %)	40 ml	$\frac{40\,ml}{1000\,ml} \times 20\,ml = 0.8\,ml$
Purified Water	25 ml	$\frac{25\,ml}{1000\,ml} \times 20\,ml = 0.5\,ml$
Peppermint Oil	4 ml	$\frac{4\,ml}{1000\,ml} \times 20\,ml = 0.08\,ml$ $= app. 2\ drops$
Glycerol (Glycerin) to	1000 ml	20 ml

Procedure: Required quantity of Potassium Iodide is dissolved in water. Iodine is dissolved in the solution of Potassium Iodide by stirring.
The peppermint oil is dissolved separately in alcohol. The peppermint oil solution is added to the iodine solution.

The resultant solution is mixed with sufficient glycerine to make the required volume.

Storage: Storage in a cool place is recommended.

Category: Throat Paint

Discussion: Throat paints are viscous due to glycerine content and they stick & adhere to the affected site. This prolongs the action of the medicament. The bottle should be shaken as some of the oils may separate on storage.

Questions and Answers:

1. What are the uses of each component of Compound Iodine Paint?

   Answer:
   - Iodine is the active ingredient (Antimicrobial),
   - Potassium Iodide is to solubilise Iodine in water,
   - Alcohol is to dissolve Peppermint Oil.
   - Peppermint Oil is the flavour.
   - Glycerine is viscous vehicle.

2. What is the use of Compound Iodine Paint?

   Answer: It is used in the treatment of pharyngitis and tonsillitis.

3. What patient guidance is required while dispensing Compound Iodine Paint?

   Answer:
   - Shake the bottle before Use.
   - Apply to the throat using the applicator supplied.
   - Dot swallow in large amount.
   - Keep in cool place.

CHAPTER - 9

Emulsions

Emulsions (as dosage forms) are liquid preparations for oral use. They are o/w emulsions and are a convenient means of administering oils or oily solutions of unpalatable drugs. (In physical term, emulsion is a disperse system where one liquid is dispersed in another liquid with which it is immiscible. The emulsified system has application for internal as well as for external use.)

The emulsion dosage form offers advantages like better acceptability (palatable), more digestible, easily absorbable or more effective. Being dispersed system, they are required to have instruction "Shake Well Before Use". They need to be measured using the supplied spoon to avoid inaccuracy of dose. The domestic measures' (spoons) capacity varies widely and hence it is recommended to use supplied measuring spoon or device. If they are suspension, the bottles need to be shaken before measuring the dose.

Though various emulsifying agents are available for use in preparing oral emulsions (o/w emulsions for internal use), acacia gum is generally used for extemporaneously prepared emulsions. A primary emulsion is first prepared using a fixed ratio of oil, water and gum and the primary emulsion is then diluted to required volume with vehicle.

The formula for primary emulsions in parts [Oil: Water: Gum] –

Fixed Oils (Arachis Oil, Castrol Oil, Cod Liver Oil) – 4: 2:1

Mineral Oil (Liquid Paraffin) – 3:2:1

Volatile Oil (Peppermint Oil, Cinnamon Oil) – 2:2:1

The oils and water are measured by volume (ml) and gum by weight (g) for making primary emulsions.

Experiment - 24

Liquid Paraffin Emulsion

Objective: To prepare and dispense 60 ml Liquid Paraffin Emulsion.

Principle: The liquid paraffin emulsion is formulated with acacia as emulsion. Acacia amount prescribed in the formula is one-fourth of the oil content. This is less than the usually required for mineral oil emulsion (one-third). This less quantity is compensated by addition of secondary emulsifying agent, tragacanth. Chloroform and sodium benzoate are included as preservatives. The emulsion is flavoured with vanillin.

While preparing, a primary emulsion is to be made first and to which other ingredients may be added and diluted to the required volume.

Formula

Ingredients	Master Formula	Working Formula	Formula for Primary Emulsion
Liquid paraffin	500 ml	$\frac{500\ ml}{1000\ ml} \times 60\ ml = 30\ ml$	Liquid Paraffin = 30 ml Water = 15 ml
Acacia, in powder	125 g	$\frac{125\ ml}{1000\ ml} \times 60\ ml = 7.5\ g$	Acacia = 7.5 g Tragacanth = 300 mg
Tragacanth	5 g	$\frac{5\ g}{1000\ ml} \times 60\ ml = 0.3\ g = 300\ mg$	
Sodium benzoate	5 g	$\frac{5\ g}{1000\ ml} \times 60\ ml = 0.3\ g = 300\ mg$	Note: Chloroform is no longer used in internal preparations and hence not used in the preparation.
Vanillin	0.5 g	$\frac{0.5\ g}{1000\ ml} \times 60\ ml = 0.03\ g = 30\ mg$	
Glycerine	125 ml	$\frac{125\ ml}{1000\ ml} \times 60\ ml = 7.5\ ml$	0.1 % Sodium Benzoate can be used as presser-vative.
Chloroform	2.5 ml	$\frac{2.5\ ml}{1000\ ml} \times 60\ ml = 0.15\ ml$	
Purified water q.s. to	1000 ml	60 ml	

Procedure: Liquid paraffin is measured accurately in a dry measure and drained into a large perfectly dry mortar. Acacia and tragacanth powders are dispersed in oil by trituration. 15 ml of water measured and added at once (in one quantity) to the mortar containing dispersed gums in oil with trituration. The trituration is continued in one direction only until primary emulsion is formed. The appearance of crackling sound is an indication of formation of primary emulsion.

The primary emulsion is slightly diluted and transferred to a measure. Vanillin and sodium benzoate are dissolved in mixture of glycerine and 3 ml of water. This solution is then added with mixing. Finally volume is adjusted adding sufficient purified water.

Storage: It should be stored in a well closed container in a cool place, but not to be kept in refrigerator.

Category: Laxative.

Dose: 8 to 30 ml.

Discussion: The method described in the procedure is called Dry Gum Method. The emulsion can also be prepared by Wet Gum Method. Though care is necessary like measuring the oil in dry measure and use of complete dry pestle and mortar, dry gum method yields better emulsion compared to wet gum method. Methyl cellulose can also be used in place of gums to prepare the liquid paraffin emulsion.

Questions and Answers

1. What are the uses of each ingredients of the formula?

   Answer: Liquid paraffin is the medicament; acacia is primary emulsifying agent; tragacanth is secondary emulsifying agent; chloroform and sodium benzoate are preservatives; glycerine and vanillin are sweetening and flavouring agents. Water is the vehicle.

2. What is the use of liquid paraffin emulsion?

   Answer: This is useful as laxative in treating constipation.

3. Why is liquid paraffin used in emulsified form?

   Answer:

   (i) The emulsified form is more effective than pure liquid paraffin.

   (ii) The taste of liquid paraffin is improved making it more palatable.

(iii) Pure liquid paraffin has problem of anal leakage. This is avoided in emulsified form.

4. What patient guidance is required while dispensing this liquid paraffin emulsion to patients?

Answer:

- Shake well before use.
- Measure the dose using supplied spoon or measuring devise.
- Preferably take at bed time.
- Store in a cool place but not in refrigerator. [Keeping in refrigerator would break the emulsion.]

Experiment - 25

Cod Liver Oil Emulsion

Objective: To prepare and dispense 50 ml Cod Liver Oil Emulsion for a 2 year old child.

Principle: Cod liver oil is a source of vitamin A and vitamin D. To improve its palatability as well to improve the absorption, cod liver oil is prepared as emulsion for use. The emulsion can be prepared using acacia as emulsifying agent and cod liver oil is treated as fixed oil for calculating the formula for primary emulsion. Tragacanth may be included as secondary emulgent to increase stability. The preparation may suitably be flavoured and sweetened.

While preparing, a primary emulsion is to be made first and to which other ingredients may be added and diluted to the required volume.

Formula

<table>
<tr><th>Ingredients</th><th>Master Formula</th><th>Working Formula</th><th>Formula for Primary Emulsion</th></tr>
<tr><td>Cod liver oil</td><td>100 ml</td><td>$\frac{100\ ml}{200\ ml} \times 50\ ml = 25\ ml$</td><td rowspan="7">Cod Liver Oil = 25 ml
Water = 12.5 ml
Acacia = 6.25 g
Tragacanth = 375 mg

Note: Chloroform is no longer used in internal preparations and hence not used in the preparation.
0.1% Sodium Benzoate can be used as presser-vative.</td></tr>
<tr><td>Acacia powder</td><td>25 g</td><td>$\frac{25\ g}{200\ ml} \times 50\ ml = 6.25\ g$</td></tr>
<tr><td>Tragacanth powder</td><td>1.5 g</td><td>$\frac{1.5\ g}{200\ ml} \times 50\ ml = 0.375\ g = 375\ mg$</td></tr>
<tr><td>Benzaldehyde spirit</td><td>0.5 ml</td><td>$\frac{0.5\ ml}{200\ ml} \times 50\ ml = 0.125\ ml$</td></tr>
<tr><td>Saccharin sodium</td><td>0.02 g</td><td>$\frac{0.02\ g}{200\ ml} \times 50\ ml = 0.005\ g = 5\ mg$</td></tr>
<tr><td>Chloroform</td><td>0.5 ml</td><td>$\frac{0.5\ ml}{200\ ml} \times 50\ ml = 0.125\ ml$</td></tr>
<tr><td>Purified water q.s. to</td><td>200 ml</td><td>50 ml</td></tr>
</table>

Procedure: Cod liver oil is measured accurately in a dry measure and drained into a perfectly dry large mortar. Acacia and tragacanth powders are dispersed in oil by trituration. 12.5 ml of water measured and added at once to the mortar containing dispersed gums in oil with trituration. The trituration is continued in one direction only until primary emulsion is formed. The appearance of crackling sound is an indication of formation of primary emulsion.

The primary emulsion is slightly diluted and transferred to a measure. Saccharin sodium and benzyldehyde spirit are added with stirring. Finally volume is adjusted adding sufficient purified water.

Storage: It should be stored in a well closed container in a cool place, but not to be kept in refrigerator.

Category: Source of vitamin A and vitamin D

Dose: This is an unofficial preparation and hence no fixed dose specified. 5 ml daily is acceptable dose.

Discussion: The method described in the procedure is called Dry Gum Method. The emulsion can also be prepared by Wet Gum Method. Though care is necessary like measuring the oil in dry measure and use of complete dry pestle and mortar, dry gum method yields better emulsion compared to wet gum method.

Questions and Answers

1. What are the uses of each ingredients of the formula?

   Answer: Cod liver oil is the medicament; acacia is primary emulsifying agent; tragacanth is secondary emulsifying agent; chloroform is preservative. Benzaldehyde spirit and saccharin are flavouring and sweetening agents. Water is the vehicle.

2. What is the use of cod liver emulsion?

   Answer: This is a source of vitamin A and D. Vitamin A is necessary for good eyesight and Vitamin D is necessary for healthy growth of bones and teeth.

3. Why is cod liver oil given in emulsified form?

   Answer:

   (i) The emulsified form is better absorbed (better effective).

   (ii) The taste of cod liver oil is improved making it more palatable.

   Now a days the cod liver capsules are available but are not suitable for children.

4. What patient guidance is required while dispensing this cod liver oil emulsion to patients?

Answer: The mother or care giver is instructed

- Shake well before use.
- Measure the dose using supplied spoon or measuring devise.
- Do not double dose. Excess vitamins may be harmful.
- Store in a cool place but not in refrigerator. [Keeping in refrigerator would break the emulsion.]

CHAPTER - 10

Powders and Granules

The powders are thorough mixtures of dry finely divided drug(s) with or without excipient(s) which are meant for either internal or external use. Internally they can be taken orally, administered through nose as snuffs, or blown into a body cavity as insufflations. Externally they can be used as dusting powders for application over the skin. The powders can also be used to dissolve in water for oral or external application.

Oral powders may be divided into two types: Bulk (undivided) powders and divided powders. The oral bulk powders are usually simple mixture of medicaments without excipients. This requires the patient to measure quantity of each dose using the supplied measuring device. The oral divided powders contain one or more medicaments with or without diluents. The diluents are required to make a minimum dose quantity to 120 mg. For divided powders, the individual dose is separately weighed and dispensed as unit dose.

The dusting powders may contain one or more medicaments usually with inert diluents like talc. They need to be very fine and free flowing for application to the skin. The dusting powders intended for application to open wounds or raw surfaces must be sterilized.

The powder dosage forms are less frequently used as oral unit dosage forms. But they continue to have their popularity as dusting powders. Oral rehydration salts (ORS) is a common example of oral powder dosage form, but are used after dissolving in prescribed quantity of water. The oral powders are being completely replaced by tablets and capsules.

While mixing of powders, the geometric dilution method is followed. The following steps are recommended:

- Adding the lowest bulk ingredient to the mortar.
- Adding a quantity of the second ingredient that approximately doubles the bulk already in the mortar.
- Mixing by trituration.

- Adding the quantity that approximately doubles the bulk already in the mortar. At each addition, the quantity that doubles the bulk in mortar is used.
- Mixing after each addition.

Experiment - 26

Oral Rehydration Salts (Oral Divided Powder)

Objective: To prepare and dispense 2 packets of Oral Rehydration Salts (ORS), each for making 200 ml solution.

Principle: The ORS is a mixture of sodium chloride, potassium chloride, sodium bicarbonate (or, sodium citrate) and anhydrous glucose. The ingredients are mixed in mortar by trituration and each unit is to be packed separately. A slight excess is required as there will be some losses due adherence to pestle and mortar. The entire amount can't be transferred from the mortar.

Formula

Ingredients	Master Formula [for 1000 ml]	Working Formula [for 200 ml]	Working Formula taking 10% extra [2 packets each for 200 ml]
Sodium chloride	2.6 g	$\frac{2.6\ g}{1000\ ml} \times 200\ ml = 0.52\ g$	1.04 g + 10% = 1.144 g
Potassium chloride	1.5 g	$\frac{1.5\ g}{1000\ ml} \times 200\ ml = 0.3\ g$	0.6 g + 10% = 0.66 g = 660 mg
Sodium citrate	2.9 g	$\frac{2.9\ g}{1000\ ml} \times 200\ ml = 0.58\ g$	1.16 g + 10% = 1.276 g
Glucose, anhydrous	13.5 g	$\frac{13.5\ g}{1000\ ml} \times 200\ ml = 2.7\ g$	5.4 g + 10% = 5.94 g
Total Quantity	20.5 g	4.1 g	
Each packet should have 4.1 g powders meant for dissolving in 200 ml water			

Procedure: Potassium chloride is mixed with sodium citrate in a mortar. Then sodium chloride is mixed. Finally glucose is mixed by trituration.

The mixed powders are passed through a sieve number 60 [250 μm] and lightly mixed. 4. 1 g powder mix is weighed and packed as one packet.

[The mixing of powders in mortar should be done in order of increasing bulk]

Storage: It should be stored in a well closed packet in a dry place.

Category: Rehydrating agent and electrolyte replenisher in diarrhoea.

Dose: Depending on extent of dehydration.

Adult: 200-400 ml solution after every loose stool.

Discussion: ORS may be prepared with sodium bicarbonate [2.5 g/Litre] substituting sodium citrate. But such formula has limited stability and is recommended for immediate use only. Similarly, in absence of glucose sucrose (common sugar) may be used 27 g/Litre].

Accurate weighing and thorough mixing of ingredients are important consideration while making ORS extemporaneously. Use of more concentrated solution (resulting from inaccurate formula) may lead to hypernatraemia (high plasma concentration of sodium).

Questions and Answers

1. What are the uses of each component of the ORS?

   Answer: Glucose facilitates the absorption sodium and water. Sodium chloride and potassium chloride are needed to supply sodium and potassium to replace the body losses during diarrhoea and vomiting. Citrate corrects the acidosis that occurs as a result of diarrhoea and dehydration.

2. What is the use of ORS?

   Answer: This is a life saving medicine. It provides rehydration and electrolyte replacement in the treatment of diarrhoea.

3. What patient guidance is required while dispensing ORS to the patients?

   Answer:

   - Prepare the solution freshly dissolving the contents in 200 ml of recently boiled and cooled drinking water.
   - Take as much as you want (patient feels like taking).

- Discard the unused portion after 24 hours. Do not use the solution that is made before 24 hour.
- This is not for reducing or curing diarrhoea but to rehydrate and prevent dehydration and supply electrolytes. Loss of electrolytes and dehydration cause life threatening situation.
- Too frequent drinking may cause vomiting.

Experiment - 27

Zinc, Starch and Talc Dusting Powder

Objective: To prepare and dispense 20 g Zinc, Starch and Talc Dusting Powder.

Principle: This is mixture of Zinc Oxide, Starch and Talc. The mixing is carried out using geometric dilution method.

Formula

Ingredients	Master Formula [for 1000 g]	Working Formula [for 20 g]
Zinc oxide	250 g	$\frac{250\ g}{1000\ g} \times 20\ g = 5\ g$
Starch, in powder	250 g	$\frac{250\ g}{1000\ g} \times 20\ g = 5\ g$
Purified Talc, Sterilized	500 g	$\frac{500\ g}{1000\ g} \times 20\ g = 10\ g$

Procedure: Zinc oxide and starch powder are mixed in a mortar. Then sterilized talc is added and mixed by trituration. The mixed powders are passed through a fine sieve [sieve no. 80 or 100], lightly mixed and packed.

[The mixing of powders in mortar should be done in order of increasing bulk]

Storage: It should be stored in a well closed screw capped plastic container with perforated lid.

Category: Adsorbent dusting powder.

Discussion: The dusting powders should not be used on acute weeping skin conditions because they can cake on the lesions, form a crust. This may promote secondary infection. Sterilized talc is used as talc is often contaminated with pathogenic microorganisms.

The product should be labelled with "For External Use Only".

Questions and Answers

1. What are the uses of each component of the Zinc, Starch and Talc Dusting Powder?

   Answer: All three substances are adsorbent. Additionally the zinc oxide is astringent.

2. What is the use of this dusting powder?

   Answer: This is used to allay irritation and prevent chaffing. They are applied to absorb the moisture especially where skin rubs the skin like between the toes or buttocks, in the arm pits or groin, or under the breasts. They dry the skin which is softened and damaged by moisture and reduce friction by absorbing moisture.

3. What patient guidance is required while dispensing Zinc, starch and Talc Dusting Powder to the patients?

   Answer:

   - Dust the powder lightly into the affected area. Do not apply to the broken skin area or raw skin surface.
   - Keep it in a dry place.

Experiment - 28

Powder Containing Eutectic Substances

Objective: To prepare and dispense 20 g of this bulk powder (formula given below) for external use.

Principle: Menthol and camphor are solids but when mixed together they become liquid mass. Any of the two methods can be used to prepare free flowing powders:

(a) Mixing of camphor and menthol separately with adsorbent before mixing them together.

(b) Mixing the resultant liquid mass with the adsorbent.

Formula

Ingredients	Master Formula [App for 40 g]	Working Formula [App for 20 g]
Menthol	100 mg	$\frac{100\ \text{mg}}{40\ \text{g}} \times 20\ \text{g} = 50\ \text{mg}$
Camphor	200 mg	$\frac{200\ \text{mg}}{40\ \text{g}} \times 20\ \text{g} = 100\ \text{mg}$
Zinc stearate	800 mg	$\frac{800\ \text{mg}}{40\ \text{g}} \times 20\ \text{g} = 400\ \text{mg}$
Zinc oxide	8 g	$\frac{8\ \text{g}}{40\ \text{g}} \times 20\ \text{g} = 4\ \text{g}$
Talc	31 g	$\frac{31\ \text{g}}{40\ \text{g}} \times 20\ \text{g} = 15.5\ \text{g}$

Procedure: Menthol and camphor are mixed together in mortar to make liquid. Zinc stearate, zinc oxide and talc are mixed by geometric dilution. The powder mixture is added to the liquid mass by geometric dilution and then mixed well by trituration.

[The mixing of powders in mortar should be done in order of increasing bulk]

Storage: It should be stored in a well closed plastic container with perforated lid.

Category: Anti-pruritic dusting powder.

Discussion: Some low melting point solids may become sticky or pasty or even liquefy when mixed and powdered. These substances are called eutectics. Camphor, menthol, phenol, thymol and chloral hydrate are few examples of eutectic substance. The mixture of these eutectics is called eutectic mixture. Two methods are suggested for developing free flowing powders from the eutectic mixtures:

(a) Separately mixing each ingredient with a small amount of diluent (adsorbent like Magnesium Oxide or Magnesium Carbonate) and then lightly combining these two mixtures. Mortar and pestle are to be avoided as they compress the powders leading to more problems.

(b) Mixing or triturating the eutectic substances to make a liquid mass which is then mixed with enough adsorbents to make it free flowing.

The dusting powders should not be used on acute weeping skin conditions because they can cake on the lesions, form a crust. This may promote secondary infection. Sterilized talc is used as talc is often contaminated with pathogenic microorganisms.

The product should be labelled with "For External Use Only".

Questions and Answers

1. What are the uses of each component of this formulation?

   Answer: Camphor and menthol are medicaments. Zinc stearate is lubricant and improves flow properties. Zinc oxide and talc are adsorbents which make the liquid mass into free flowing powder. Talc has good flow property.

2. What is the use of this dusting powder?

   Answer: This is used as antipruritic dusting powder. Its medicaments (camphor and menthol) provide relief to itching. Due to their cooling effect, the dusting powder provides soothing touch to the skin. This helps the patient avoid scratching the skin and possibly prevent secondary bacterial infection.

3. What patient guidance is required while dispensing this Dusting Powder to the patients?

Answer:

- Dust the powder lightly into the affected area. Do not apply to the broken skin area or raw skin surface.
- Keep it in a dry place.

Experiment - 29

Powder Containing Explosive Substances

Objective: To prepare and dispense 2 packets of powder (formula given below) for use as gargle. [This experiment need not be performed but just be discussed.]

Principle: Potassium chlorate may react violently when mixed with tannic acid and sucrose. Special care is necessary while combining them. They need to be mixed lightly.

Formula

Ingredients	Master Formula [App for one packet]	Working Formula [App for 2 packets]
Potassium chlorate	600 mg	600 mg × 2 = 1.2 g
Tannic acid	300 mg	300 mg × 2 = 600 mg
Sucrose	300 mg	300 mg × 2 = 600 mg

Procedure: Potassium chlorate, tannic acid and sucrose are separately powdered preferably in perfectly cleaned separate mortar and pestle. Separate mortar and pestle are used to prevent the mixing of even little of one ingredient with other while trituration. Then these three substances are lightly mixed in a sheet of paper. Then each dose is weighed and supplied in paper pack.

Storage: It should be stored in a dry place.

Category: Antiseptics and astringents for gargle.

Discussion: Potassium chlorate is an oxidizing agent. Tannic acid and sucrose are reducing agents. When mixed together especially triturated, there would be oxidation-reduction reaction causing violent explosion. Many accidents due to vigorous mixing have been reported.

The product should be labelled with "Not to be swallowed".

Questions and Answers

1. What are the uses of each component of this formulation?

   Answer: Potassium chlorate is antiseptic and astringent. Tannic acid is astringent. The sugar is to make gargle tastier for use.

2. What is the use of this preparation?

   Answer: This preparation is no longer in use. It was earlier used as powder for gargle. The powder was meant for dissolving in drinking water and gargling for the treatment of sore throat. Even the potassium chlorate tablets were available to allay irritation and quickly restoring cleanness to the voice.

3. What patient guidance is required while dispensing this powder for gargle to the patients?

   Answer: This preparation is no longer used due to its explosive nature. However, the following instructions are essential:

   - Do not carry in pant pocket or handbag. The mixing during travelling may cause explosion.
   - Keep it in a dry place.
   - Do not try to mix the powders. It may cause explosion.
   - Do not swallow the materials while gargling.

Experiment - 30

Menthol Insufflation [Powder for Inhalation]

Objective: To prepare and dispense 25 g of menthol insufflation (formula given below).

Principle: Menthol and camphor are solids but when mixed together they become liquid mass. Any of the two methods can be used to prepare free flowing powders:

(a) Mixing of camphor and menthol separately with adsorbent before mixing them together.

(b) Mixing the resultant liquid mass with the adsorbent.

Ammonium chloride is hygroscopic and tends to absorb moisture. The preparation is to be stored in air tight container.

Formula

Ingredients	Master Formula [for 100 g]	Working Formula [for 25 g]
Menthol	5 g	$\frac{5\ g}{100\ g} \times 25\ g = 1.25\ g$
Camphor	5 g	$\frac{5\ g}{100\ g} \times 25\ g = 1.25\ g$
Ammonium Chloride	30 g	$\frac{30\ g}{100\ g} \times 25\ g = 7.5\ g$
Magnesium Carbonate	60 g	$\frac{60\ g}{100\ g} \times 25\ g = 15\ g$

Procedure: The required quantity of menthol, camphor and ammonium chloride are mixed by trituration to form a liquid mass. The light magnesium carbonate is mixed with the liquid mass following geometric dilution. The final product would be free flowing and passed through a fine sieve.

The product is dispensed in an air tight container.

Storage: It should be stored in a well closed container in a cool and dry place.

Category: Decongestant, for nasal use.

Discussion: Insufflations are fine powders intended for inhalation from suitable insufflator. These medicated powders are blown into ear, nose or throat by means of a device called insufflator. The product should be labelled with "Not to be swallowed" and "For Nasal Use Only".

Questions and Answers

1. What are the uses of each component of this formulation?

   Answer: Camphor is soothing agent and rubefacient. Menthol is soothing agent and counter irritant. Ammonium chloride is expectorant. Magnesium carbonate is adsorbent diluent to adosorb the liquefied mass that results from mixing of menthol and camphor.

2. What is the use of this preparation?

   Answer: It is used to relieve nasal congestion. [Though useful, they are being replaced by better drugs and formulations like nasal spray or nasal drops]. At present the inhalation powder is enclosed in hard gelatine capsule. After insertion into the insufflator or rotahaler, the shells get broken or pierced. The flow of released powder is controlled by patient's own respiratory effort.

3. What patient guidance is required while dispensing this insufflation to the patients?

   Answer:

   - Sniff at every 2 hours.
   - Do not take internally.

Experiment - 31

Compound Effervescent Powder BPC [Seidlitz Powder] [Oral Divided Powder]

Objective: To prepare and dispense 2 doses of Compound Effervescent Powder.

Principle: Sodium Potassium Tartrate Powder is the medicament but the quantity per dose is high (7.5 g). The powder is too large to be swallowed as single dose. Hence, it is formulated to dissolve in water prior to swallowing. The powder is supplied in two packets and when they are mixed produces effervescence. The combination of sodium bicarbonate and tartaric acid in presence of water react and produce effervescence. The quantity of tartaric acid is slightly more than required to neutralize sodium bicarbonate.

Formula

<table>
<tr><th>Ingredients</th><th>Master Formula for One Dose</th><th rowspan="6">Working Formula (No separate calculation needed as the dose is to be prepared individually and quantity for one dose can be easily weighed)</th></tr>
<tr><td colspan="2">Powder 1</td></tr>
<tr><td>Sodium Potassium Tartrate Powder</td><td>7.5 g</td></tr>
<tr><td>Sodium Bicarbonate</td><td>2.5 g</td></tr>
<tr><td colspan="2">Powder 2</td></tr>
<tr><td>Tartaric Acid Powder</td><td>2.5 g</td></tr>
</table>

Procedure: The components of powder 1 are weighed and mixed. The mixed powder is wrapped in blue paper.
The component of powder 2 is weighed and wrapped in white paper.
Powder 1 and Powder 2 together is one dose.

Storage: Protect from high humidity.

Category: Saline purgative.

Dose: One of each powder.

Discussion: This powder is also known as 'Seidlitz Powder' as the original formula was intended to represent the chief saline constituent of Seidlitz spring in Czechoslovakia.

Traditionally, the powder 1 is packed in blue paper and power 2 is packed in white powder for easy identification. The powder 2 should be added only after the content of powder 1 is dissolved. Otherwise, there is possibility of missing some quantity of sodium potassium tartrate (medicament).

Though the contents of powder 1 and powder 2 are of different quantity, it is preferable to have both packets of same size.

It is better to double wrap both the powders using waxed paper as inner wrapper. This is to prevent contact with water.

Questions and Answers:

1. What are the uses of each component of Compound Effervescent Powder?
   Answer: Sodium potassium tartrate is the medicament. Sodium bicarbonate and Tartaric acid react in presence of water to produce effervescence. The effervescent preparation would be morc plcasing as it masks the undesirable taste.
2. What is the use of Compound Effervescent Powder?
   Answer: It is used in constipation.
3. What patient guidance is required while dispensing Compound Effervescent Powder?
   Answer:
   - Dissolve the content of powder 1 (blue paper) in a tumblerful of cold water. Add the content of powder 2 (white powder), stir and take while the mixture is still effervescing.
   - Follow the order of mixing.

Experiment - 32

Sodium Phosphate Effervescent Granules

Objective: To prepare and dispense 30 g Sodium Phosphate Effervescent Granules.

Principle: Sodium phosphate has saline and unpleasant taste. The unpleasant taste is masked by preparing it in the form of effervescent product. The effervescence is due to reaction of citric acid and tartaric acid with sodium bicarbonate.

The granules are prepared by moistening the mass and passing through appropriate sieve. The moistening water is obtained from liberation of water of crystallization and water produced during reaction between tartaric acid and sodium bicarbonate.

$$3\ NaHCO_3 + C_6H_8O_7.H_2O \rightarrow C_6H_5Na_3O_7 + 3CO_2 \uparrow + 3H_2O$$

Sodium Citric acid Sodium Citrate

Bicarbonate

$$3\ NaHCO_3 + C_4H_6O_6 \rightarrow C_4H_4Na_2O_6 + 2CO_2 \uparrow + 2H_2O$$

Sodium Tartaric acid Sodium Tartrate

Bicarbonate

Formula

Ingredients	Master Formula (for 1091 g)	Working Formula for 40 g (taking 10 g extra to dispense the required quantity)
Sodium Phosphate, dried and powdered	200 g	$\frac{200\ g}{935\ g} \times 40\ g = 8.55\ g$
Sodium bicarbonate, dry	477 g	$\frac{477\ g}{935\ g} \times 40\ g = 20.4\ g$
Tartaric acid, dry	252 g	$\frac{252\ g}{935\ g} \times 40\ g = 10.8\ g$
Citric acid, monohydrate	162 g	$\frac{162\ g}{935\ g} \times 40\ g = 6.93\ g$
Assuming loss of one-seventh quantity during preparation, this may produce 935 g.		To produce 40 g

Procedure:

i. The powdered citric acid is mixed with dried sodium phosphate and tartaric acid. Sodium bicarbonate is added to the above mixture and mixed gently.
ii. A porcelain dish is heated on water bath. The powder mixture is placed on the heated porcelain dish. The powder mixture is mixed with help of spatula till the whole mass becomes damp. This may take few minutes.
iii. The damp mass is passed through sieve number 20. The granules so produced is dried in hot air oven not exceeding 60 °C.
iv. The dried granules are packed in a wide mouthed jar.

Storage: Storage in a cool dry place is recommended (Avoid contact with water). Wide mouth jar is preferred for ease of measuring dose by the patient.

Category: Saline Purgative.

Dose: 2 to 16 g.

Discussion: The loss of weight occurs during preparation due to: evaporation from the damp mixture; and loss of carbon dioxide. This loss equals to approximately one-seventh of powder used and this should be taken into account while deciding the quantity to be used for dispensing the desired quantity.

The porcelain dish must be hot enough to ensure rapid liberation of water of crystallization from the citric acid. The water must be boiling in the water bath. This is an indicator of hotness of porcelain dish. If the heating is delayed until the powder is placed in the dish, the water is liberated slowly as the temperature rises but much is lost by evaporation. This is an issue of getting sufficient water for moistening.
Sucrose may be included as sweetening agent.

Questions and Answers:

1. What are the uses of each component of Sodium Phosphate Effervescent Granules?

Answer:

- Sodium Phosphate is the active ingredient (Saline Purgative).
- Sodium bicarbonate, Citric acid and Tartaric acid are effervescence causing agents.

2. What is the use of Sodium Phosphate Effervescent Granules?
   Answer: Saline purgative.
3. Why are effervescent granules preferred over effervescent powders?
   Answer: The powders produce uncontrolled effervescence because of quick reaction (powders have more surface area) which may lead to overflowing / spillage. The granules will have controlled effervescence and would be easier for the patients to take while effervescing.
4. What patient guidance is required while dispensing Sodium Phosphate Effervescent Granules?
   Answer:
   - Add the dose into half tumblerful of drinking water (do not use complete tumblerful) and drink while effervescing,
   - Keep in cool dry place. Avoid contact with water prior to use.

CHAPTER - 11

Liniments

Liniments are liquid or semi-liquid preparations meant for external application with friction. They are either solutions or emulsions. They contain medicaments possessing analgesic, rubefacient, soothing or stimulating properties.

In general, the alcoholic or hydroalcoholic products are useful as rubefacient and counter irritant while oleaginous liniments are used when massage is needed. They should be applied to the skin with considerable friction by massaging with hand.

Liniments should not be applied to broken or bruised skin as the preparation may cause excessive irritation.

Experiment - 33

Turpentine Liniment IP [1966]

Objective: To prepare and dispense 50 ml Turpentine Liniment.

Principle: Turpentine oil is not soluble in water and it needs emulsification. The soft soap is used as emulsifying agent.

Formula

Ingredients	Master Formula	Working Formula
Soft soap	90 g	$\frac{90\text{ g}}{1000\text{ ml}} \times 50\text{ ml} = 4.5\text{ g}$
Camphor	50 g	$\frac{50\text{ g}}{1000\text{ ml}} \times 50\text{ ml} = 2.5\text{ g}$
Turpentine Oil, freshly rectified	650 ml	$\frac{650\text{ ml}}{1000\text{ ml}} \times 50\text{ ml} = 32.5\text{ ml}$
Purified water q.s. to	1000 ml	50 ml

Procedure: The required quantity of soft soap is mixed with 5 ml of purified water in a mortar. Camphor is dissolved in turpentine oil. The camphor solution is then gradually added to soap and water mixture with trituration until a thick creamy emulsion is formed. This emulsion is transferred to the calibrated bottle and finally enough water is added to make up the volume to 50 ml.

A More Practical Method: Soap and camphor are triturated in a mortar. Oil is added in small amount at a time, mixing well after each addition. When all the lumps are dispersed, the rest of the oil may be added quickly.

The coarse dispersion is transferred into a beaker as it is easier to pour small quantity from the beaker than mortar. The required quantity of water (one-third of oil) is taken in a calibrated bottle [to the volume to be made, in this case it is 50 ml]. The oily suspension already prepared and kept in the beaker is added in small quantity to the bottle vigorously shaking after each addition.

Finally enough purified water is added to make up the volume.

[Shaking a soap emulsion produces froths; this air needs to be removed before adjustment of volume. It is essential to leave the preparation for an hour or two for escaping of the air.]

Storage: It should be stored in a well closed container.

Category: Counter Irritant and Rubefacient.

Discussion: The Turpentine Liniment is o/w emulsion prepared using an alkali soap as emulsifying agent. Turpentine oil and camphor are the active medicaments with rubefacients and counter irritant properties. The preparation should be stored in cool place but not to be frozen.

They should be stored in glass bottles. The plastics are to be avoided as turpentine reacts with some plastics.

Questions and Answers

1. What is the percentage of turpentine oil in this liniment?

   Answer: Turpentine oil content is 65 % (v/v).

2. A liquid preparation is a solution, suspension or emulsion. The turpentine emulsion belongs to which type?

   Answer: It is emulsion of o/w type. Soft soap is emulsifying agent.

3. What is the use of turpentine liniment?

   Answer: It is useful to provide relief from rheumatic pain, and sore muscle.

4. What guidance is necessary for the patients?

   Answer:

   - For external use only. Must not be taken internally.
   - Do not apply to the broken or bruised skin. Do not use near the eyes or mucous membranes.
   - Shake well before use.
   - Apply with rubbing or massaging.
   - Keep away from reach of children.

Experiment - 34

Camphor Liniment BPC

Objective: To prepare and dispense 50 ml Camphor Liniment.

Principle: Camphor Liniment is a solution of camphor in a vegetable oil.

Formula

Ingredients	Master Formula	Working Formula
Camphor	200 g	$\frac{200\ g}{880\ ml} \times 50\ ml =$ app 11.5 g
Arachis oil	800 g = app equal to 880 ml	50 ml

Procedure: The required quantity of camphor is dissolved in 50 ml of Arachis oil in a closed vessel.

Storage: It should be stored in air tight container in a cool place.

Category: Counter Irritant.

Discussion: Camphor is the medicament dissolved in a oily vehicle (arachis oil).

Questions and Answers

1. What is the percentage of camphor in this liniment?

   Answer: The camphor content is 20 % (w/w); or app 12 % (v/v).

2. A liquid preparation is a solution, suspension or emulsion. The camphor liniment belongs to which type?

   Answer: It is an oily solution.

3. What is the use of camphor liniment?

   Answer: It is useful as counter irritant in the treatment of fibrositis (where fibres of muscles of neck, shoulders and back etc. are inflamed) and neuralgia. It is useful for relieving pain at muscles and joints.

4. What guidance is necessary for the patients?

Answer:

- For external use only. Must not be taken internally.
- Do not apply to the broken or bruised skin. Do not use near the eyes or mucous membranes.
- Apply with rubbing or massaging.
- Keep away from reach of children.

CHAPTER - 12

Lotions

Lotions are liquid preparations meant for external application to the skin. They are intended to provide protective or therapeutic value of their constituents. They are intended to dry on the skin soon after application leaving a thin coat of the medicaments on the skin surface.

The most common vehicles of lotions are aqueous. They are made either as suspensions or emulsions. Since the dispersed phase gets separated over time on standing, they need to be shaken well before use for uniform mixing. The label must bear such instructions for the patients.

Experiment - 35

Calamine Lotion IP [1966]

Objective: To prepare and dispense 50 ml Calamine Lotion.

Principle: Calamine Lotion is a suspension of calamine and other ingredients in rose water with bentonite as suspending agent. Liquefied phenol and glycerine are added to get antiseptic and humectant properties respectively.

Formula

Ingredients	Master Formula	Working Formula
Calamine	150 g	$\frac{150\ g}{1000\ ml} \times 50\ ml = 7.5\ g$
Zinc Oxide	50 g	$\frac{50\ g}{1000\ ml} \times 50\ ml = 2.5\ g$
Bentonite	30 g	$\frac{30\ g}{1000\ ml} \times 50\ ml = 1.5\ g$
Sodium Citrate	5 g	$\frac{5\ g}{1000\ ml} \times 50\ ml = 0.25\ g = 250\ mg$
Liquefied Phenol	5 ml	$\frac{5\ ml}{1000\ ml} \times 50\ ml = 0.25\ ml$
Glycerin	50 ml	$\frac{50\ ml}{1000\ ml} \times 50\ ml = 2.5\ ml$
Rose water of commerce q.s. to	1000 ml	50 ml

Procedure: The required quantity of calamine, zinc oxide and bentonite are triturated in a porcelain mortar with a solution of sodium citrate in 35 ml of rose water. Liquefied phenol and glycerine are added to this. Finally sufficient rose water is added to make the volume 50 ml.

[The transfer of the suspension from the measuring cylinder to the container is not easy. Complete transfer is not possible. Hence the adjustment of volume is advisable in calibrated bottle in which the product is to be supplied].

Storage: It should be stored in a well closed container in a cool place.

Category: Protective.

Discussion: Calamine is chemically zinc oxide with a small proportion of ferric oxide. The presence of ferric oxide gives the pink colour of calamine. The pink colour helps the lotion to match with fair skin colour on application and thereby make the preparation more cosmetically acceptable. Additional zinc oxide maintains the required concentration of zinc oxide in the lotion to provide the desired protective action.

For dark skin persons, calamine can be completely substituted with Zinc Oxide.

Bentonite is a suspending agent which helps the dispersion of insoluble ingredients in rose water. Glycerine promotes adherence of the residual powders on the skin surface. It also keeps the skin moist on application due to its humectant property. Besides it increases the stability of suspension due to increased viscosity.

Liquefied phenol has antiseptic and local anaesthetic properties. It also serves as preservative for the product. The inclusion of it enhances the antipruritic (anti-itching) activity of the lotion. Sodium citrate maintains the proper consistency of the suspension for easy pourability. Also, it prevents excessive frothing on shaking of the lotion.

Questions and Answers

1. What are the uses of each ingredients of the formula?

   Answer: Calamine and zinc oxide are protective (active ingredients). Though calamine and zinc oxide are pharmacologically (action wise) same, use of calamine gives the pink colour to the lotion which helps in matching with fair pink skin. The pink colour thus helps disguise the presence of lotion on the skin.

   Bentonite is a suspending agent. Sodium citrate causes partial deflocculation of calamine and transforms the bentonite from gel to sol. The absence of sodium citrate would make the suspension much thicker and difficult to pour from the bottle. It helps preventing excessive frothing on shaking.

   Glycerine has multiple functions: keeps the skin moist, promotes adherence of residual powder on skin surface and improves stability due to increase in viscosity. Liquefied phenol is anti-pruritic and preservative. Rose water is a perfumed vehicle.

2. What are the uses of calamine lotion?

   Answer: The calamine lotion is protective with good drying effect and mild astringent. On application to the skin, the water evaporates leaving a residue of medicaments on the skin. The lotion is useful in relieving itching and pain of sunburn, insect stings, and other minor skin irritations.

3. What patient guidance is required while giving this calamine lotion to patients?

   Answer:

   - Do not use on weeping, vesicular lesions. [The repeated application of the lotion will cause deposition of dry solids forming cake. This would occlude the area and promote bacterial growth]. If required for use for long periods, the skin should be cleansed of dried crusts prior to each application.
   - Shake the bottle before each use.
   - For external use only.

Experiment - 36

Benzyl Benzoate Lotion USP

Objective: To prepare and dispense 30 ml Benzyl Benzoate Lotion.

Principle: Benzyl Benzoate Lotion is an emulsion of benzyl benzoate in water. The soap formed *in situ* is used as emulsifying agent.

Formula

Ingredients	Master Formula	Working Formula
Benzyl Benzoate	250 ml	$\frac{250\text{ ml}}{1000\text{ ml}} \times 30\text{ ml} = 7.5\text{ ml}$
Triethanol Amine	5 g	$\frac{5\text{ g}}{1000\text{ ml}} \times 30\text{ ml} = 0.15\text{ g} = 0.13\text{ ml}$ [wt/ml is 1.12 g]
Oleic acid	20 g	$\frac{20\text{ g}}{1000\text{ ml}} \times 30\text{ ml} = 0.6\text{ g} = 0.67\text{ ml}$ [wt/ml is 0.895 g]
Purified water	750 ml [to make 1000 ml product]	$\frac{750\text{ ml}}{1000\text{ ml}} \times 30\text{ ml} = 22.5\text{ ml}$ [to make about 30 ml]

Procedure: Triethanol amine and oleic acid are mixed in a beaker. Benzyl benzoate is added and mixed.

The mixture is transferred to a suitable container which is about double the size of the required volume to be manufactured [here it is 60 ml). One third of the required water (here it is 7.5 ml) is added. The mixture is shaken thoroughly.

Finally remaining water is added and the product is shaken thoroughly.

Storage: It should be stored in a well closed container in a cool place.

Category: Scabicide and pediculocide.

Discussion: The emulsifying agent, an organic soap, is prepared *in situ* by combining two liquid ingredients: oleic acid and triethanol amine.

$$(HOCH_2CH_2)_3N + C_{17}H_{33}COOH \rightarrow (HOCH_2CH_2)_3NH\text{-}OOC\ (C_{17}H_{33})$$

Triethanol amine   Oleic acid   Triethanol amine oleate

During preparation (after addition of water), the mixture is shaken in an oversized container to ensure thorough agitation. Amine soap products (triethanol amine oleate) darken on standing. They should be stored away from light and out of contact with metals. Heavy metals accelerate discolouration.

Questions and Answers

1. What are the uses of each ingredients of the formula?

   Answer: Benzyl benzoate is the medicament (for scabies and pediculosis), triethanol amine and oleic acid interact to form triethanol amine oleate as emulsifying agent, and water is the vehicle.

2. What are the uses of benzyl benzoate lotion?

   Answer: The lotion is used externally in the treatment of scabies and pediculosis.

3. What patient guidance is required while giving this benzyl benzoate lotion to patients?

   Answer:

   - For scabies: Apply to cleaned but still damp skin (except face).
   - Allow the lotion to remain on the skin for about 24 hours. Then wash off thoroughly.
   - Shake the bottle before each use.
   - For external use only.

CHAPTER - 13

Suppositories

The suppositories are solid medicated dosage forms intended for insertion to rectum, vagina or urethra. They melt or dissolve on insertion and provide either local or systemic action. The vaginal suppositories are also known as pessaries and urethral suppositories are known as bougies.

They are effective means of administering medicines to infants and children, to severely debilitated patients to whom oral medication cannot be given. The suppositories too serve as alternative to parenteral medications.

Examples of suppositories for local action: treatment of haemorrhoids, itching, infection and constipation.

Examples of suppositories for systemic action: treatment of nausea and vomiting, asthma, and fever.

The suppositories are prepared extemporaneously by pouring the molten mass to suitable moulds. The shape of the moulds decides the shape of the suppositories. They should be individually wrapped when extemporaneously prepared and dispensed in tight glass or plastic container.

The important feature of the suppositories is that they are solid at room temperature but melts at body temperature (37°C). While the temperature often going above 37°C, it is necessary to store them in refrigerator. Accordingly the products are to be labelled.

Experiment - 37

Boric Acid Suppositories

Objective: To prepare and dispense 3 suppositories each containing 120 mg boric acid.

Principle: Boric acid suppositories are prepared with theobroma oil as base. The displacement value of boric acid is 1.5 with respect to theobroma oil. This is taken into account while calculating the base required. The displacement value of the medicament is the number of parts by weight of the medicament that displaces one part by weight of the base.

Formula

Ingredients	Master Formula [for 1 suppository]	Working Formula [taking 3 extra suppositories = 6 suppositories]	Base required for 6 suppositories
Boric acid	120 mg	720 mg	1.5 g boric acid displaces 1 g of base
Theobroma oil q.s. to	1 g	6 g	0.72 g of boric acid would displace; $\frac{1\ g}{1.5\ g} \times 0.72 = 0.48\ g$; The amount of base required = $6\ g - 0.48\ g = 5.52\ g$

Procedure: The suppository mould is cleaned and lubricated. The lubricated mould is inverted over ice cube to drain excess lubricant and cool the mould. [The soap based lubricant with the formula: soft soap – 1 g, glycerine -1 ml and rectified spirit – 5 ml is recommended for lubrication when fatty base is used].

The required quantity of shredded theobroma oil (5.52 g) is heated in a china dish over a water bath until two-third of the base is melted. Then the china dish is removed from the heating source. This would avoid over heating but the remaining base will melt automatically with that heat.

The finely powdered required quantity of boric acid is mixed with half of melted base on a warm tile using a flexible spatula. Then the boric acid mixed base is quickly transferred to the melted base in china dish and mixed to make homogenous mixture.

When the mixture is about to thicken, the mass is poured into the chilled mould taking care to overfill each cavity. Over filling is necessary as there will be contraction on cooling leading to depression.

On solidification the excess is trimmed off horizontally using a sharp knife. Then the suppositories are removed, wrapped individually and supplied.

Storage: It should be stored in a tight container in a cool place.

Category: Antiseptic.

Discussion: The overheating of theobroma oil is to be avoided. The overheating leads to formation of unstable polymorphs of base which would not solidify quickly. In a country like ours where room temperature is very high, it is necessary to add white beeswax to raise the softening point. The product should be labelled with "For Rectal Use Only".

Questions and Answers

1. What are the uses of each component of the Boric acid suppositories?

   Answer: Boric acid is the medicament. Cocoa butter is the suppository base.

2. What is the use of Boric acid suppositories?

   Answer: The Boric acid suppositories are used in the treatment of proctitis (inflammation of rectum and anus), anal-cryptitis (inflammation) and anal fissures. [Boric acid as antiseptic is used to keep the rectal and anal area clean and prevent infection]. Boric acid vaginal suppositories are used to treat yeast infection and fungal infection like candidiasis. But they are available as capsules.]

3. What is the use of displacement value in making suppositories?

   Answer: The volume of suppository mould is fixed but the weight of the suppository would vary depending upon the density of the base and the medicament. Usually the weight of suppository expressed is based on theobroma oil base. For calculating the quantity of base the displacement value (quantity of base displaced by the medicament) is used. This is important when it is necessary to prepare suppositories each containing fixed quantity of the medicament. However, displacement value has no significance when the medicament is expressed as percentage.

4. What patient guidance is required while dispensing boric acid suppositories to the patients?

Answer:

- Keep the suppositories in refrigerator. Outside temperature may often be too high. The suppositories may melt.
- After removing the suppository from refrigerator, unwrap and moisten with water before inserting into rectum.
- If too soft, chill it before insertion.
- Insert to about 2.5 cm to 5 cm in infants and children. [Insert to 2.5 cm in adults].
- Wash your hands thoroughly before and after insertion.
- Avoid defecation for at least one hour after insertion.
- For Rectal Use Only. Not to be swallowed.

Experiment - 38

Choral Hydrate Suppositories

Objective: To prepare and dispense 3 suppositories each containing 60 mg chloral hydrate for a child.

Principle: Chloral hydrate reduces the melting point of theobroma oil making the preparation of suppositories difficult. Such products are often too soft to handle. But the amount of chloral hydrate used in each suppository is too low to cause a significant change in base's properties. The displacement value of chloral hydrate is 1.5. This should be considered for calculating the quantity of base.

Formula

Ingredients	Master Formula [for 1 suppository]	Working Formula [for 6 suppositories]	Quantity of base required
Chloral hydrate	60 mg	360 mg	1.5 g chloral hydrate displaces 1 g of base 0.72 g of chloral hydrate would displace; $\frac{1\ g}{1.5\ g} \times 0.72 = 0.48$ g;
Theobroma oil q. S. to	1 g	6 g	The amount of base required = 6 g – 0.48 g = 5.52 g

Procedure: The suppository mould is cleaned and lubricated. The lubricated mould is inverted over ice cube to drain excess lubricant and cool the mould. [The soap based lubricant with the formula: soft soap – 1 g, glycerine -1 ml and rectified spirit – 5 ml is recommended for lubrication when fatty base is used].

The required quantity of shredded theobroma oil (5.52 g) is heated in a china dish over a water bath until two-third of the base melted. Then the china dish is removed from the heating source. This would avoid over heating but the remaining base will melt automatically with that heat.

The finely powdered required quantity of chloral hydrate is mixed with half of melted base on a warm tile using a flexible spatula. Then the boric acid mixed base is quickly transferred to the melted base in china dish and mixed to make homogenous mixture.

When the mixture is about to thicken, the mass is poured into the chilled mould taking care to overfill each cavity. Over filling is necessary as there will be contraction on cooling leading to depression.

On solidification the excess is trimmed off horizontally using a sharp knife. Then the suppositories are removed, wrapped individually and supplied.

Storage: It should be stored in a tight container in a cool place.

Category: Sedative.

Dose: One at night.

Discussion: The overheating of theobroma oil is to be avoided. The overheating leads to formation of unstable polymorphs of base which would not solidify quickly. In a country like ours where room temperature is very high, it is necessary to add white beeswax to raise the softening point. The product should be labelled with "For Rectal Use Only".

Questions and Answers:

1. What are the uses of each component of the Chloral hydrate suppositories?

   Answer: Chloral hydrate is the medicament. Cocoa butter (Theobroma oil) is the suppository base.

2. What is the use of chloral hydrate suppositories?

   Answer: This is used for the treatment of insomnia, to relieve anxiety and induce sleep prior to surgery. Chloral hydrate has now been replaced by newer medicines.

3. What patient guidance is required while dispensing chloral hydrate suppositories to the patients?

   Answer:

   - Keep the suppositories in refrigerator. Outside temperature may often be too high. The suppositories may melt.
   - After removing the suppository from refrigerator, unwrap and moisten with water before inserting into rectum.
   - If too soft, chill it before insertion.
   - Insert to about 2.5 cm to 5 cm in infants and children. [Insert to 2.5 cm in adults].

- Wash your hands thoroughly before and after insertion.
- Avoid defecation for at least one hour after insertion.
- For Rectal Use Only. Not to be swallowed.

Experiment - 39

Glycero - Gelatin Suppositories

Objective: To prepare and dispense 3 child's size Glycerol-Gelatin Suppositories.

Principle: Glycero-Gelatin Base is 1.2 times denser than the theobroma oil base (cocoa butter). But the capacities of the suppositories moulds are stated based on the theobroma oil. The total quantity of the base required should be multiplied by 1.2 to get the required quantity of glycerol-gelatin base.

The base (in this case also medicament) is prepared by dissolving gelatine in boiling water and then mixing with hot glycerine (100°C).

Calculation: Considering for 3 extra suppositories as there would be substantial manipulative loss:

The quantity of base required = 2 g × 6 suppositories = 12 g [the child's size suppositories = 2 g]

Taking the density consideration, the quantity of glycerol-gelatin base required = 12 g × 1.2 = 14.4 g = App 15 g

Formula

Ingredients	Master Formula [App for 100 g]	Working Formula [App for 15 g]
Gelatin	14 g	$\frac{14\ g}{100\ g} \times 15\ g = 2.1\ g$
Glycerol	70 g	$\frac{70\ g}{100\ g} \times 15\ g = 10.5\ g = 8.75$ ml taking specific gravity of glycerol 1.2
Purified Water to make	100 g	15 g

Procedure: The required quantity of glycerin is heated in a dish to 100°C.

About 4.5 ml purified water (it is slightly higher than required which can be adjusted later) is taken in a tared dish and heated to boiling and removed from source of heating. The gelatine powder is added to this hot water with stirring to dissolve. The gelatine solution may be kept heating but charring to be avoided.

The hot glycerol is added to the gelatine solution and the solution is stirred until homogenous. The stirring should be gentle to avoid entrapment of air bubbles.

Then weight is adjusted either by evaporation or by adding hot water (and mixing). The molten mass is poured into the previously lubricated mould to fill. [The lubrication of the mould can be done by applying liquid paraffin to the inner surface of the mould with the help of muslin. After lubrication the mould is closed and inverted on a clean tile to drain excess lubricant.]

The molten mass is allowed to set (solidify). On solidification the suppositories are removed, wrapped individually and supplied.

Storage: It should be stored in tight container in a cool temperature protecting from humidity/moisture.

Category: Laxative.

Discussion: The glycerol-gelatin suppositories are to be stored at dry condition. Otherwise due to hygroscopicity they absorb moisture and loose shape and consistency. Due to hygroscopicity of glycerine these suppositories cause a dehydrating effect upon insertion. Hence they are moistened with water prior to insertion. Moistening helps in insertion too due to lubricating effect.

Though this preparation is used as laxative, the formula can be used as base for the preparation of medicated suppositories.

The product should be labelled with “For Rectal Use Only”.

Questions and Answers

1. What are the uses of each component of this formulation?

   Answer: Glycerin is the medicament and gelatine to make the product solid. Water is for mixing (gelling of gelatine).

2. What is the use of Glecero-Gelatin Suppositories?

   Answer: This is used to treat constipation in children (also in adults). This is also used as base for preparing medicated suppositories.

3. What patient (mother of the child) guidance is required while dispensing these suppositories?

   Answer:

   - Remove the wrapper and moisten with water before insertion into rectum.
   - Store in refrigerator. But bring the suppositories to room temperature before insertion.
   - The child would pass motion within few minutes of insertion.
   - For Rectal Use Only. Not to be swallowed.

Experiment - 40

Zinc Oxide Suppositories

Objective: To prepare and dispense 04 Zinc Oxide Suppositories (using Cocoa Butter as Base).

Principle: The displacement value of Zinc Oxide is 5 with respect to Cocoa Butter. This is taken into account while calculating the base required. The displacement value of the medicament is the number of parts by weight of the medicament that displaces one part by weight of the base.

Formula

Ingredients	Master Formula (for 1 Suppository)	Working Formula (for 6 Suppositories, taking 2 extra)	Base required for 6 Suppositories
Zinc Oxide	400 mg	400 mg × 6 = 2.4 g	5 g Zinc Oxide displaces 1 g of base; 2.4 g Zinc Oxide would displace $\frac{1\,g}{5\,g} \times 2.4\,g =$ $0.48\,g$; The amount of base required = 6 g – 0.48 g = 5.52 g
Cocoa Butter q. s. to	1 g	6 g	

Procedure: The suppository mould is cleaned and lubricated. The lubricated mould is inverted over ice cube to drain excess lubricant and cool the mould. [The soap-based lubricant with the formula: soft soap – 1 g, glycerine -1 ml and rectified spirit – 5 ml is recommended for lubrication when fatty base is used].

The required quantity of shredded Cocoa Butter (5.52 g) is heated in a China dish over a water bath until two-third of the base is melted. Then the China dish is removed from the heating source. This would avoid over heating but the remaining base will melt automatically with that heat.

The finely powdered required quantity of Zinc Oxide is mixed with half of melted base on a warm tile using a flexible spatula. Then the Zinc

Oxide mixed base is quickly transferred to the melted base in China dish and mixed to make homogenous mixture.

When the mixture is about to thicken, the mass is poured into the chilled mould taking care to overfill each cavity. Over filling is necessary as there will be contraction on cooling leading to depression.
On solidification the excess is trimmed off horizontally using a sharp knife. Then the suppositories are removed, wrapped individually and supplied.

Storage: Store in a cool place.

Category: Astringent.

Discussion: The overheating of Cocoa Butter (Theobroma oil) is to be avoided. The overheating leads to formation of unstable polymorphs of base which would not solidify quickly. In a country like ours where room temperature is very high, it is necessary to add white beeswax to raise the softening point. The product should be labelled with "For Rectal Use Only".

Questions and Answers:

1. What are the uses of each component of Zinc Oxide Suppository?
   Answer: Zinc Oxide is Astringent (Medicament);
   Cocoa Butter is base.
2. What is the use of Zinc Oxide Suppository?
   Answer: It is used to relieve burning, pain and itching caused by haemorrhoids.
3. What is the use of displacement value in making suppositories?

   Answer: The volume of suppository mould is fixed but the weight of the suppository would vary depending upon the density of the base and the medicament. Usually, the weight of suppository expressed is based on Theobroma oil base. For calculating the quantity of base, the displacement value (quantity of base displaced by the medicament) is used. This is important when it is necessary to prepare suppositories each containing fixed quantity of the medicament. However, displacement value has no significance when the medicament is expressed as percentage.

4. What patient guidance is required while dispensing Zinc Oxide Suppository?

Answer:

- Keep the suppositories in refrigerator. Outside temperature may often be too high. The suppositories may melt.
- After removing the suppository from refrigerator, unwrap and moisten with water before inserting into rectum.
- If too soft, chill it before insertion.
- Insert to about 2.5 cm to 5 cm in infants and children. [Insert to 2.5 cm in adults].
- Wash your hands thoroughly before and after insertion.
- Avoid defecation for at least one hour after insertion.
- For Rectal Use Only. Not to be swallowed.

CHAPTER - 14

Ointments and Other Semi Solid Preparations

Ointments, creams, pastes and gels are semisolid preparations for application to the skin. Ointments should spread easily and free from grittiness. Ointments are usually greasy, anhydrous and immiscible with skin secretion. Creams are viscous emulsions of semi-solid consistency intended for application to the skin. Creams are cosmetically more appealing. Pastes are stiffer preparations than ointments and contain high proportion of powders. Gels are transparent or translucent, non-greasy, aqueous preparations for application to the skin.

The decision on use of typical topical preparation depends on: how much skin penetration of medicament is needed and on the characteristics of skin. Ointments are generally used on dry, scary lesions which requires emollient effect. Creams are applied to moist and weeping lesions. They provide a drying effect as lesions fluids are miscible with aqueous external phase. Pastes are applied to the area which requires protection. Gels are used as dermatological bases or as lubricants for catheters and gloves. There are gels for ophthalmic use too and ophthalmic preparations need to be sterile.

Containers: The screw capped amber coloured glass or plastic pots or collapsible pots can be used. Plastic containers are to be avoided for preparations containing methyl salicylate as the latter dissolves plastics. The ointments should be packed neatly with top surface as smooth as possible.

They need to be stored in a cool place. The additional details of labelling, storage and counselling points are given under each preparation.

Experiment - 41

Sulphur Ointment B.P. [1980]

Objective: To prepare and dispense 20 g Sulphur Ointment.

Principle: Sulphur Ointment is the dispersion of Sulphur in Absorption Ointment Base. Simple Ointment prepared with White Soft Paraffin is the Absorption Ointment base. Finely divided Sulphur is dispersed by levigating with the base.

Formula for Sulphur Ointment:

Ingredients	Master Formula	Working Formula
Precipitated Sulphur, finely sifted	100 g	$\frac{100\ g}{1000\ g} \times 20\ g = \ 2.0\ g$
Simple Ointment prepared with White Soft Paraffin	900 g	$\frac{900\ g}{1000\ g} \times 20\ g = \ 18.0\ g$
Total	1000 g	20 g

Formula for Simple Ointment:

Ingredients	Master Formula	Working Formula
Wool Fat	50 g	$\frac{50\ g}{1000\ g} \times 20\ g = \ 1.0\ g$
Hard Paraffin	50 g	$\frac{50\ g}{1000\ g} \times 20\ g = \ 1.0\ g$
Cetostearyl Alcohol	50 g	$\frac{50\ g}{1000\ g} \times 20\ g = \ 1.0\ g$
White Soft Paraffin	850 g	$\frac{850\ g}{1000\ g} \times 20\ g = \ 17.0\ g$
Total	1000 g	20 g

Procedure:

I. Preparation of Simple Ointment:

The hard paraffin is grated and the required quantity is weighed. The weighed quantity is placed in an evaporating dish (China dish) on a water bath for melting. The required quantities of other ingredients are added to the melted mass and mixed gently by stirring. When homogeneous, it is removed from the heat and stirred until cold. The molten base can be kept for preparation of Sulphur Ointment.

II. Preparation of Sulphur Ointment:

The required quantity of sifted Sulphur is placed on a large ointment tile. The powder is levigated with about two times weight of the base. Gradually more bases are added and mixed until homogenous.

Storage: It should be supplied in wide mouthed amber jar with a grease proof disc.

Category: Mild Antiseptic

Discussion: The patient should be advised to cleanse the area prior to application. The ointment should be sparingly applied. After application, hand should be washed.

Questions and Answers:

1. What are the uses of each ingredient of the formula?
   Answer: Sulphur is the active ingredient (antibacterial). Wool Fat, Hard Paraffin, Cetostearyl Alcohol and white Soft Paraffin are the components of ointment base. This ointment base is called absorption base (capacity to absorb water – wool fat is the main component for absorption). Other ingredients are to get the semisolid consistency.

2. What is the use of Sulphur Ointment?
   Answer: It can be used to treat acne and scabies

3. What patient guidance is required while giving this Sulphur Ointment?

   Answer:

   - Apply sparingly over the cleaned skin.
   - Wash hands after use of this medicine.
   - For external use only.

Experiment - 42

Non-Staining Iodine Ointment with Methyl Salicylate BPC

Objective: To prepare and dispense 20 g Non-Staining Iodine Ointment with Methyl Salicylate.

Principle: Elemental Iodine stains skin and clothes. Combined Iodine with double bonds of unsaturated free acids do not stain.

$CH_3.(CH_2)_7.CH = CH.(CH_2)_7.COOH + I_2 \rightarrow CH_3.(CH_2)_7.CHI.CHI.(CH_2)_7.COOH$

(Oleic Acid) (Di-iodo Oleic Acid)

Methyl Salicylate is incorporated into non-staining iodine ointment.

Formula

Ingredients	Master Formula	Working Formula
Iodine	50 g	$\frac{50\,g}{1000\,g} \times 20\,g = 1\,g$
Arachis Oil	150 ml	$\frac{150\,ml}{1000\,g} \times 20\,g = 3\,ml$
Yellow Soft Paraffin qs to	1000 g	$20\,g$ (Approximate quantity 17 g)
Methyl Salicylate	50 g	1 g = 1.17 ml (based on density)

Procedure:

Preparation of Non-Staining Iodine Ointment:

Iodine is finely powdered in a glass mortar and required quantity is added to Arachis Oil taken in glass stoppered conical flask (the conical flask may be too big, a glass test tube is adequate). The mixture is stirred well.

This is heated at 50 °C on a thermostatically controlled water bath with occasional stirring. The heating is continued till the brown colour becomes greenish black. This iodised oil is added and mixed with warm / melted yellow soft paraffin of 40 °C. This is non-staining iodine ointment.

[It is preferable to determine the iodine content before mixing other components so as to maintain iodine content as there is possibility of loss of iodine during heating. However, for extemporaneous preparation, this can be avoided].

Incorporation of Methyl Salicylate: The methyl salicylate is measured and mixed with required quantity of non-staining iodine ointment.

Storage: It should be stored in a well closed container in a cool place.

Category: Local analgesic

Discussion: It is dark, greenish black preparation. When rubbed into the skin, the active ingredients are readily absorbed.

Methyl Salicylate is a volatile liquid. Liquids are easier to measure than weighing. The small quantity of liquid required in the preparation is better measured.

Plastic containers are not to be used as they get dissolved in methyl salicylate.

Questions and Answers:

1. What are the uses of cach ingredient of the formula?

   Answer: Iodine and methyl salicylate are active ingredients. Arachis oil (other names: peanut and ground nut oil) provide unsaturated acids for reaction with Iodine. The combined iodine becomes non-staining.

2. Why is it called Non-Staining?

   Answer: Iodine stains the skin and clothes. The combined Iodine with unsaturated fatty acid of arachis oil, do not stain when rubbed into the skin.

3. What is the use of Non-Staining Iodine Ointment with Methyl Salicylate?

   Answer: It is used for treatment of pain in rheumatic condition.

4. What patient guidance is required while giving this non-staining iodine ointment with methyl salicylate to patients?

   Answer:

   - Apply with massage.
   - Do not use on broken / inflamed skin. Do not use near the eyes.
   - Wash your hand after each use.
   - For external use only.

Experiment - 43

Dimethicone Aqueous Gel

Objective: To prepare and dispense 50 g Dimethicone Aqueous Gel (Prepared with Carbomer).

Principle: Carbomer is used as gelling agent to produce clear gel. Carbomer is first dispersed in water and propeller may be used locating close to the bottom of the mixing vessel to minimise incorporating air into the preparation. After removal of the entrapped air, other ingredients are to be added. The neutralizing agent is added to thicken the gel.

Formula

Ingredients	Master Formula (for 100 g)	Working Formula (for 50 g)
Dimethicone copolyol	2.3 g	$\frac{2.3\ g}{100\ g} \times 50\ g = \ 1.15\ g$
Carbomer 934	0.5 g	$\frac{0.5\ g}{100\ g} \times 50\ g = \ 0.25\ g$ = 250 mg
Triethanolamine	1.2 g	$\frac{1.2\ g}{100\ g} \times 50\ g = \ 0.6\ g$ = 0.5 ml (taking 1.1 g/ml as density)
Glycerin	34.2 g	$\frac{34.2\ g}{100\ g} \times 50\ g = \ 17.1\ g =$ $14.25\ ml\ (taking\ 1.2\frac{g}{ml} as\ density)$
Propylene glycol	2 g	$\frac{2\ g}{100\ g} \times 50\ g = \ 1\ g =$ $1\ ml\ (taking\ 1\frac{g}{ml}\ as\ density)$
Sodium hydroxide	1 g	$\frac{1\ g}{100\ g} \times 50\ g = \ 0.5g$
Purified Water	59.8 g	$\frac{59.8\ g}{100\ g} \times 50\ g = \ 29.9\ g = 29.9\ ml$

Procedure: Carbomer is dispersed in 10 ml purified water. pH of the dispersion is adjusted to 7 by addition of sodium hydroxide (about 6 ml 1 % sodium hydroxide is needed). The enough purified water is added to make 20 ml.

Other ingredients are added and mixed well.

Storage: Store in air tight container in a cool place.

Category: Skin protective.

Discussion: Care should be taken to prevent incorporation too much air, otherwise it would not be a clear gel. The clear gels are consumer appealing.
The equipments (after preparation of carbomer gel) are easily cleaned by using warm water containing salt, detergent, and sodium hydroxide.

Questions and Answers:

1. What are the uses of each ingredient of the formula?
   Answer:
   - Dimethicone copolyol: Active ingredient (medicament);
   - Carbomer 934: Gelling agent;
   - Triethanolamine: Alkalising agent;
   - Glycerin: Vehicle;
   - Propylene glycol: Vehicle;
   - Sodium hydroxide: Alkalising agent;
   - Purified water: Vehicle.
2. What are the uses of Dimethicone Aqueous Gel?

   Answer: It is useful as protective barrier on the skin preventing the entry of irritants. It prevents the moisture loss from the skin and is used to prevent or treat dry, rough, scaly, itchy skin and minor skin irritations. It keeps the skin hydrated, soft and supple.
3. What patient guidance is required while giving this Dimethicone Aqueous Gel to patients?

   Answer:
   - Apply to the affected areas of the skin.
   - Do not apply on sensitive areas: eyes, mouth, nose, vagina, groin area or broken skin.
   - For external use only.

CHAPTER - 15

Incompatibilities

When two or more antagonistic substances are mixed together for making a formulation and the mixing reflects the appearance, safety or efficacy of the final product, an incompatibility is said to have occurred. As most of the pharmaceutical products are manufactured by pharmaceutical companies, the practicing pharmacists have very little role in compounding. The pharmaceutical companies solve the issue of incompatibilities while developing the products.

Though need of developing extemporaneous preparations are less, the basic understanding of various incompatibilities always help pharmacists to manipulate the prepared products when necessary especially developing paediatric dose when they are commercially not available or preparing intravenous admixtures. The knowledge of the incompatibilities helps avoiding therapeutic problems.

The incompatibilities can be classified into: Pharmaceutical Incompatibility and Therapeutic Incompatibility. The pharmaceutical incompatibility is further divided into Physical Incompatibility and Chemical Incompatibility. The pharmaceutical incompatibility occurs when the components of the formulation react with each other physically or chemically to give an undesirable product.

The examples of physical incompatibility are: immiscibility (mixture of oil and water), insolubility (liquid preparation containing insoluble solids), and liquefaction (mixture of solids results in liquid mass).

The examples of chemical incompatibility are: oxidation-reduction reaction (potassium chlorate and sugar), hydrolysis (aspirin and water), precipitation (alkaloidal salts and alkaline solution) and complexation (salicylic acid in macrogol ointment base – reduction in release rate).

Therapeutic incompatibility is usually the responsibility of the physicians. But it is also the pharmacist's professional responsibility to avoid them in the interest of patient's safety. Therapeutic incompatibility may result in no effect to harming the patient. Examples of therapeutic incompatibility are: dosing error (over or under dosing), contraindicated medication (ampicillin to penicillin allergic patient), synergistic (liver toxicity of paracetamol and alcohol) or antagonistic effect (tetracycline with milk). The drug interactions are the most common form of therapeutic incompatibility especially when a patient takes several medications together, a condition called polypharmacy.

The exercises given under this chapter are not meant for preparing or dispensing. They are just discussed to identify and avoid the incompatibility.

Experiment - 44

Physical Incompatibility [Insolubility]

Objective: To identify the incompatibility in the given formula and suggest method to overcome the same.

Formula:

Magnesium carbonate	– 7.5 g
Sodium bicarbonate	– 15 g
Citric acid	– 15 g
Purified water to	500 ml
Make a solution.	

Incompatibility Identified: Insolubility of Magnesium carbonate in water. This is a physical incompatibility.

Method(s) to overcome: Citric acid and sodium bicarbonate are soluble in water. But the magnesium carbonate is not soluble. Two methods are available to correct this incompatibility:

1. The final appearance of the product depends on the order of mixing.

   If sodium bicarbonate is first dissolved in a solution of citric acid and then magnesium carbonate is added, it would not produce a solution. Some of the magnesium carbonate will remain un-dissolved.

   On the other hand, simply changing the order of mixing would result in a clear solution. The method to be followed: The citric acid is first dissolved in water. To this solution magnesium carbonate is added and the carbonate would get dissolved. Later the sodium bicarbonate can be dissolved.

2. This can be prepared as suspension using a suspending agent. However, the product is to be shaken well before measuring each dose. The additional label "Shake Well Before Measuring Each Dose" is necessary.

   Use of the Preparation: This is a gastric antacid.

Discussion: Insolubility occurs because of the inability of the ingredients to get dissolved in the solvent system or due to precipitation. The following methods are available to overcome this insolubility problem:

- Adjusting the solvent system.
- Changing the order of mixing.
- Use of suspending agent.
- Substitution of ingredient(s).

Questions and Answers

1. What is physical incompatibility?

   Answer: Physical incompatibility is the problem posed by the physical properties of the ingredient(s) in a formulation or preparation of the product (without any chemical reaction involved) resulting unsightly and non-uniform product which is difficult to use.

2. What are the various types/examples of physical incompatibilities?

   Answer: Insolubility, immiscibility and liquefaction are common physical incompatibilities. Oils are immiscible with water. If oil is the medicament (Liquid paraffin emulsion), an emulsion is to be prepared.

   Many solids are insoluble in water. Water is usually choice of solvent for pharmaceutical preparations. Calamine is insoluble (Calamine lotion) in water. A suspension is the choice. Paracetamol is insoluble in water. The problem can be addressed by making a suspension in water or solution with co-solvents.

   Liquefaction of powders occur either due to formation of eutectic mixtures or liberation of water of crystallization. They need to be mixed with adsorbent powders to make them free flowing.

3. What are the advantages of oral solutions over oral suspensions?

   Answer: Two distinct advantages:

   - Bioavailability especially the rate of absorption is higher. This leads to quick action.
   - Chance of inaccurate dosing is less. Shake well is not necessary.

4. What are gastric antacids?

   Answer: Gastric antacids are the medicines used to reduce the excess acidity in the stomach. They are not meant for absorption. They chemically neutralise the excess gastric acid in the stomach.

Experiment - 45

Physical Incompatibility [Liquefaction]

Objective: To identify the incompatibility in the given formula and suggest method to overcome the same.

Formula:

Menthol	– 100 mg
Camphor	– 200 mg
Zinc stearate	– 800 mg
Zinc oxide	– 8 g
Talc	– 31 g

Make a Dusting Powder.

Incompatibility Identified: Liquefaction due to formation of eutectic mixture (menthol + camphor). This is a physical incompatibility.

Method(s) to overcome: The liquefaction due to formation of eutectic mixture can be redressed by any of two methods:

- Mixing the powders with a bulky adsorbent like magnesium oxide or magnesium carbonate. Zinc oxide and talc can also be used. After mixing each substance with adsorbent, they are lightly mixed (not triturated). But there is a risk of not getting each ingredient powdered finely enough.
- Making the eutectic and then adsorbing the liquid mass using a bulky adsorbent.

The latter method is preferred: The menthol and camphor are powdered together to get liquid mass. The zinc stearate, zinc oxide and talc are separately mixed following geometric dilution. Then the powder is geometrically incorporated into the liquid mass with trituration. This would result a free flowing powder.

Use of the Preparation: This is an anti-pruritic dusting powder.

Discussion: The mixing of powders often leads to liquefaction. The liquefaction may be due to: formation of eutectic mixture or liberation of water of hydration. Eutectic mixture: These are few examples of substances which when powdered together result in a liquid or soft mass due to lowering of melting points below the room temperature - Aspirin,

Camphor, Chloral hydrate, Menthol, Phenol, Salicylic Acid, and Thymol. The crystalline powder that contains water of hydration is called efflorescent powder. Common examples of efflorescent powders: Alums, Atropine sulphate, Caffeine, Citric acid, Codiene, Ferrous sulphate, Sodium carbonate and Sodium phosphate. The water of hydration gets liberated either during manipulation or upon exposure to high humidity and results a sticky, pasty or liquid mass.

The efflorescent powders can be handled in two ways

1. Use of anhydrous form of the drug. The equivalent quantity of hydrated form is required.
2. Inclusion of a drying bulky powder. The light non-compacting method of mixing powder is to be followed.

Questions and Answers

1. What is physical incompatibility?

   Answer: Please refer the previous exercise.

2. What are the various types/examples of physical incompatibilities?

   Answer: Please refer the previous exercise.

3. What are eutectic mixtures?

   Answer: The eutectic mixtures are mixtures of solids which on contact turns into a liquid or pasty mass due to lowering of melting points. Menthol, thymol, camphor are common examples which form eutectic mixtures.

4. What is the need of free flowing and fine dusting powders?

   Answer: The dusting powders are meant to be used on sprinkling from the container. If they are not free flowing they cannot be properly applied over the skin.

   As they need to be applied over the skin, they need to be free from grittiness.

Experiment - 46

Chemical Incompatibility [Oxidation]

Objective: To identify the incompatibility in the given formula and suggest method to overcome the same.

Formula: Sodium salicylate - 4 g
Sodium bicarbonate - 8 g
Peppermint water sufficient to make 90 ml solution

Incompatibility Identified: Alkaline catalysed oxidation of salicylate to a quinoid form. This results in harmless change of colour to reddish brown. This is a chemical incompatibility.

Method(s) to overcome: The oxidation of salicylate causes darkening of the solution on standing but without loss of therapeutic activity. Three methods are available for overcoming this problem:

1. Addition of an antioxidant: Sodium metabisulphite at 0.1% concentration may be used to prevent the oxidative reaction.
2. Darkening the colour of the mixture: The addition of liquid liquorice extract or any other colour would mask the colour change. The patient would not be able to appreciate this change.
3. Informing patient on colour change: As the colour change is harmless and without loss of therapeutic action, the patient may be informed of this colour change. This would help patient understanding and will not bother about the colour change.

Use of the Preparation: This is an anti-pyretic preparation.

Discussion: Sodium salicylate is the medicament for relieving high temperature (antipyretic). When it comes in contact with gastric acid on taking the medicine, salicylic acid is formed. The needle shaped crystal of salicyclic acid may irritate gastric mucosa leading to lot of patient's discomfort. In order to prevent this conversion of salicylate to salicylic acid, the gastric is neutralized using sodium bicarbonate.

Questions and Answers

1. What is chemical incompatibility?

   Answer: Chemical incompatibility is the problem arises when one component reacts with another component while formulating or preparing a pharmaceutical product to produce unsuitable product.

2. What are the various types/examples of chemical incompatibilities?

   Answer: Oxidation, hydrolysis, complexation are common chemical incompatibilities encountered in pharmaceutical preparations.

   Ferrous sulphate oxidises to ineffective ferric form. The problem of oxidation is avoided by giving coating to tablets. In ferrous sulphate syrup, ascorbic acid is used to prevent oxidation.

   Hydrolysis is often catalysed by hydrogen and/or hydroxyl ions and the rate of reaction is dependent on pH of the product. Pilocarpine eye drop is stabilized by adjusting the pH at 5.0 (considering other aspects like therapeutic effect and compatibility with eyes). Insoluble form of the drug may also be used and a suspension preparation avoids hydrolysis. Procaine salt of benzyl penicillin is less susceptible to hydrolysis than benzyl penicillin.

3. Give examples of currently used antipyretics.

   Answer: Paracetamol and Ibuprofen are few antipyretics currently used.

Experiment - 47

Chemical Incompatibility [Evolution of gas]

Objective: To identify the incompatibility in the given formula and suggest method to overcome the same.

Formula:

Sodium bicarbonate	- 750 mg
Borax	- 750 mg
Phenol	- 375 mg
Glycerine	- 12.5 g
Water to	- 50 ml (solution)

Incompatibility Identified: The reaction of Glyceril – Boric acid with sodium bicarbonate liberates carbon dioxide. Glyceryl boric acid results from reaction of boric acid (results from hydrolysis of borax) with glycerine. If the product is dispensed without completing the reaction, the bottle may burst due to pressure from generated carbon dioxide. The boric acid usually does not react with bicarbonate. But in presence of glycerine, it forms glyceryl boric acid and is strong enough to react with bicarbonate. This is a chemical incompatibility.

Borax (on hydrolysis) $\rightarrow$ Boric acid)

Boric acid + Glycerine $\rightarrow$ Glyceryl Boric acid

Glycetyl Boric acid + Sodium bicarbonate $\rightarrow$ Carbon dioxide $\uparrow$

Method (s) to overcome: The reaction may be allowed to take place in an open vessel till evolution of carbon dioxide ceases. Hot water may be used to accelerate the reaction.

The sodium bicarbonate and borax are dissolved in hot water. Glycerine is added and allowed the reaction to complete. Completion of reaction would be indicated stopping of evolution of carbon dioxide. Then phenol is incorporated, mixed and volume is adjusted finally.

Use of the Preparation: This is antiseptic throat paint. Previously the borax glycerine was used as paints for the throat, tongue and mouth. Now its use is restricted due to toxicity of boric acid.

Discussion: The carbonates and bicarbonates in presence of acids stronger than carbonic acid produces carbon dioxide. The reaction needs to be completed before the product is supplied. If the reaction continues in the bottle supplied, there may be explosion or leakage.

When the reaction is slow, it should be hastened using a hot vehicle.

Questions and Answers

1. What is chemical incompatibility?

   Answer: Please refer the previous exercise.

2. What are the various types/examples of chemical incompatibilities?

   Answer: Please refer the previous exercise.

3. Why is the use of boric acid preparations are discontinued from use?

   Answer: Repeated use of boric acid preparations causes chronic boric poisoning. The main symptoms include blue-green vomit, diarrhoea, and bright red rash on the skin.

4. Give examples of currently used throat paints or similar products.

   Answer: Lot of medicated lozenges like strepsil are available for treatment of sore throat. Lignocaine – Salicylic acid paint is available for mouth and throat inflammation.

Experiment - 48

Therapeutic Incompatibility [Inappropriate Drug Selection]

Objective: To identify the therapeutic incompatibility in the given medication order (case) and suggest method to overcome the same.

Medication Order: A 5o year old person has been recently diagnosed with asthma. His medical history showed that he is known case of osteoarthritis and hypertension. He is a habitual drinker and smoker. He has been taking medicines:

Paracetamol tab – 500 mg as required

Propranolol tab – 40 mg thrice daily

Salbutamol MDI – 2 puffs every 6 hour

Budesonide dry powder inhaler – 200 microgram twice daily

Incompatibility Identified: The patient is recently diagnosed with asthma and two medications (Salbutamol and Budesonise) are given to him. The BP medicine the patient is taking currently (propranolol) has bronchospasm as one of the adverse effects. Thus propranolol is contraindicated or not to be given to bronchial asthma patients. Here the bronchial asthma is likely due to adverse effects of propranolol.

Whether the asthma identified recently is due to the drug induced or not can be validated by measuring peak expiratory flow rate.

Method(s) to overcome: The blood pressure medicine requires a change. In place of propranolol other medicines like amlodipine, enalapril etc. may be given. The treating physician is to be informed of propranolol's contraindication with bronchial asthma. The change of propranolol will avoid the need of asthma medicines.

Discussion: The beta blocker blood pressure medicines (propranolol, atenolol, carvedilol) have the bronchospasm as one of the adverse effects. They are contraindicated in asthma patients. It is necessary to ensure that this patient is not given beta blocker at any time.

Questions and Answers

1. What is therapeutic incompatibility?

   Answer: Therapeutic incompatibility is the problem that arises when a medicine contains two or more substances which are antagonistic, synergistic or additive to each other. However, the current expanded definition encompasses the use of several medicines by an individual (polypharmacy) causing drug related issues including dosing error.

2. What are the various types/examples of therapeutic incompatibilities?

   Answer: Dosing error, Wrong drug, Drug Duplication, Drug-Drug Interaction, Drug-Food Interaction are common therapeutic incompatibilities.

3. What is high blood pressure?

   Answer: When the blood pressure is more than 139/89 mm of Hg, it is called high blood pressure and the patient requires therapeutic treatment.

4. How can the problem of inappropriate drug selection / prescription be avoided?

   Answer: Several methods are suggested:

   - Limited list of medicines for use of health facilities (Essential Medicine List).
   - Clinical pharmacy service which reviews the medications.
   - Availability of Hospital formulary.
   - Provision of Drug Information Services.

Experiment - 49

Therapeutic Incompatibility [Drug - Drug Interaction]

Objective: To identify the therapeutic incompatibility in the given medication order (case) and suggest method to overcome the same.

Medication Order: A young person has reported at OP clinic with chronic sinusitis. The patient looks pale (anaemic). The past medication history: He has tried different course of ampicillin and ciprofloxacin on advice of a friend. Occasionally he takes gastric antacids. Now the doctor prescribed:

Tetracycline tablet – 500 mg four times a day

Ferrous sulphate tablet – 200 mg twice daily

Incompatibility Identified: The patient is prescribed two medications. Tetracycline is a broad spectrum antibiotic for infection and the ferrous sulphate is iron supplement for anaemia. Tetracycline combines with iron and other metallic ions to form complexes in gastrointestinal tract and forms complexes. This complex is not absorbable. Thus iron reduces the absorption of tetracycline which would reduce the antibacterial effect.

Method(s) to overcome: Ideally speaking these two medicines should not be given together. But as the patient is anaemic, Iron is required. The administration must be separated by at least two hours. The best thing is to take iron 2 hours before or 4 hours after tetracycline.

Discussion: The absorption of Tetracycline group of medicines is reduced by gastric antacids, iron, and milk and milk products. They should not be taken together. With respect to milk and milk products: take antibiotic at least one hour before or two hour after these food items. Doxicycline absorption is not affected by dairy products.

Questions and Answers

1. What is therapeutic incompatibility?

   Answer: Please refer previous exercise.

2. What are the various types/examples of therapeutic incompatibilities?

   Answer: Please refer previous exercise.

3. Give examples of any other drug-drug or drug food interaction.

   Drug-Drug Interactions

   - Liquid paraffin reduces the absorption of fat soluble vitamins – Administration at different time is suggested.
   - Warfarin (oral anticoagulant in venous thromboembolism) with Barbiturate (hypnotic) – Patient requires higher level of warfarin for therapeutic effect as liver metabolizing enzymes are induced by barbiturate. But when barbiturate is discontinued, it is necessary to reduce the dose of warfarin failing which high dose of warfarin increases the bleeding risk.

   Drug-Food Interactions

   - Grape fruit juice reacts with many medicines. It increases the simvastatin (cholesterol lowering drug) level in the blood with increased risk of muscle breakdown and kidney damage (rhabdomyolysis).
   - Alcoholic drinks (ethyl alcohol) and Metronidazole (medicine for amoebiasis) – This may lead to nausea, vomiting, headache, abdominal cramps etc. They need to be avoided using together.

4. How can the problem of drug-drug interaction be avoided?

   Answer: Several methods are suggested;

   - Each prescription needs review by clinical pharmacy service.
   - Computerized prescription where drug-drug interaction checker software is installed.
   - Limited number of medicines in the hospital list (essential medicine list).

Experiment - 50

Therapeutic Incompatibility [Dosing Error]

Objective: To identify the therapeutic incompatibility in the given medication order (case) and suggest method to overcome the same.

Medication Order: A child is undergoing treatment for leukaemia in a cancer hospital. The doctor orders for 30 mg of hydralazine intravenously every 6 hour for treating emergency hypertension.

Incompatibility Identified: The dose of hydralazine is very high. This is a prescription error of wrong dose. This is the adult dose. High dose if administered, may lead to severe hypotension and even cardiac arrest.

Method(s) to overcome: It is necessary to confirm again from the treating physician. The physician should be told of this dosing error. Perhaps the dose asked is 3.0 mg [A decimal point missing].

Discussion: Dosage calculation is important especially when potent medications are given to children. Often this is one of the causes of medication error. The pharmacist needs to validate the dose based on mg/kg body weight or using body surface area formula. A proper care is necessary while writing the dose especially if it involves a decimal point.

Questions and Answers

1. What is therapeutic incompatibility?

   Answer: Please refer the earlier exercise.

2. What are the various types/examples of therapeutic incompatibilities?

   Answer: Please refer the earlier exercise.

3. Give formula used for calculating the paediatric dose.

   Answer: Two formulae are currently recommended:

   - Weight basis: mg/kg dose is converted to the requirement of the child. This just to multiply by the weight of the child in kg.

- Body surface area basis:

  Child's dose =

$$\frac{\text{Adult dose}}{1.73\,\text{m}^2} \times \text{Body surface area of the child in m}^2$$

Body surface area can be calculated from height and weight of the child.

4. Why do children require different dosing than adults?

   Answer: The physiology of children largely differs from that of adult. The metabolizing and other organs are not completely matured. These affect the drug action. The dose is not always proportionate with that of adult.

Experiment - 51

Therapeutic Incompatibility [Drug Duplication]

Objective: To identify the therapeutic incompatibility in the given medication order (case) and suggest method to overcome the same.

Medication Order: A patient with rheumatoid arthritis is given the following medications:

Piroxicam cap – 10 mg daily

Famotidine tab – 20 mg twice daily

Esomeprazole tab – 20 mg at night

Incompatibility Identified: Piroxicam is a non-steroidal anti-inflammatory drug (NSAID) used in the treatment of rheumatoid arthritis. But like other NSAIDs this causes gastric irritation and even lead to ulceration in sensitive patients. In order to prevent the gastric effects of piroxicam, the two other medications: famotidine and esomeprazole are prescribed. Though these two drugs act differently, the therapeutic effect is same. They reduce gastric acid secretion. This is the case of drug duplication (one drug would have been enough).

Method(s) to overcome: The duplication might have come by oversight. This is common when medicines are prescribed in brand name. There are many brands for same drug and this causes confusion.

Thy physician may be contacted back with a suggestion that famotidine or esomeprazole may be deleted. Famotidine may be retained and given to the patient.

Discussion: Rheumatoid arthritis is characterized by persistent inflammation of small and large peripheral joints. Most of the time symptomatic treatment is offered with NSAIDs. All NSAIDs have tendency to cause gastric irritation. But all the persons taking these medications may not need acid reducing drugs.

Questions and Answers

1. What is therapeutic incompatibility?

   Answer: Please refer the earlier exercise.

2. What are the various types/examples of therapeutic incompatibilities?

   Answer: Please refer the earlier exercise.

3. What area NSAIDs and their therapeutic effects?

   Answer: Non steroidal Anti-inflammatory Drugs analgesic, anti-inflammatory and antipyretic action. They are used to reduce both pain and inflammation in diseases like osteoarthritis.

4. What is the usefulness of the acid reducing drugs?

   Answer: The acid reducing drugs are divided into two types: H_2 Blockers (Ranitidine, Famotidine) and Proton pump inhibitors

Bibliography

1. Loyd V. Allen, Jr. (1998), The Art, Science, and Technology of Pharmaceutical Compounding, American Pharmaceutical Association, Washington, D.C.
2. Dianna M. Collett and Michael E. Aulton Edited (1991), Pharmaceutical Practice, ELBS with Churchill Livingstone, UK.
3. S. J. Carter Edited (1975), Cooper and Gunn's Dispensing for Pharmaceutical Students, Twelfth Edition, CBS Publishers and Distributors, New Delhi.
4. Howard C. Ansel *etal* (1995), Pharmaceutical Dosage Forms and Drug Delivery Systems, Sixth Edition, B. I. Waverly Pvt Ltd, New Delhi.
5. E. A. Rawlins Edited (Reprinted 2004), Bently's Textbook of Pharmaceutics, 8th Edition, All India Traveller Book Seller, Delhi.
6. Eric W. Martin Edited (1971), Dispensing of Medication, Seventh Edition, Mack Publishing Company, USA.
7. Indian Pharmacopoeia various editions.
8. British Pharmacopoeia various editions.
9. British Pharmaceutical Codex and Pharmaceutical Codex various editions.
10. WHO Model Formulary (2008), World Health Organization, Geneva, Switzerland.
11. Good Pharmacy Practice Training Manual (2005), Indian Pharmaceutical Association – Central Drug Standard Control Organization and WHO country Office for India.

www.ingramcontent.com/pod-product-compliance
Lightning Source LLC
Chambersburg PA
CBHW071225230926
51849CB00001B/27